AIMING HIGH

About Policy Network

Policy Network is an international thinktank and research institute. Its network spans national borders across Europe and the wider world with the aim of promoting the best progressive thinking on the major social and economic challenges of the 21st century.

Our work is driven by a network of politicians, policymakers, business leaders, public service professionals, and academic researchers who work on long-term issues relating to public policy, political economy, social attitudes, governance and international affairs. This is complemented by the expertise and research excellence of Policy Network's international team.

A platform for research and ideas

- Promoting expert ideas and political analysis on the key economic, social and political challenges of our age.
- Disseminating research excellence and relevant knowledge to a wider public audience through interactive policy networks, including interdisciplinary and scholarly collaboration.
- Engaging and informing the public debate about the future of European and global progressive politics.

A network of leaders, policymakers and thinkers

- Building international policy communities comprising individuals and affiliate institutions.
- Providing meeting platforms where the politically active, and potential leaders of the future, can engage with each other across national borders and with the best thinkers who are sympathetic to their broad aims.
- Engaging in external collaboration with partners including higher education institutions, the private sector, thinktanks, charities, community organisations, and trade unions.
- Delivering an innovative events programme combining in-house seminars with large-scale public conferences designed to influence and contribute to key public debates.

www.policy-network.net

AIMING HIGH

Progressive Politics in a High-Risk, High-Opportunity Era

Edited by
Florian Ranft

policy network

ROWMAN &
LITTLEFIELD
INTERNATIONAL

London • New York

Published by Rowman & Littlefield International Ltd.
Unit A, Whitacre, 26-34 Stannary Street, London, SE11 4AB
www.rowmaninternational.com

Rowman & Littlefield International Ltd. is an affiliate of Rowman & Littlefield
4501 Forbes Boulevard, Suite 200, Lanham, Maryland 20706, USA
With additional offices in Boulder, New York, Toronto (Canada), and Plymouth (UK)
www.rowman.com

British Library Cataloguing in Publication Data
A catalogue record for this book is available from the British Library

ISBN: PB 978-1-78660-099-8
eISBN: 978-1-78660-100-1

Library of Congress Cataloging-in-Publication Data
Library of Congress Control Number: 2016937535

∞ ™ The paper used in this publication meets the minimum requirements
of American National Standard for Information Sciences—Permanence of Paper
for Printed Library Materials, ANSI/NISO Z39.48-1992.

Printed in the United States of America

CONTENTS

ACKNOWLEDGEMENTS

This volume accompanies a larger series of seminars and conferences that took place in 2015 and 2016 to forge common centre-left thinking on political economy, social investment and education. They aimed to develop a reform agenda to help progressive politicians navigate key structural trends shaping western economies, such as the transition to a digital economy and political fragmentation.

We have drawn on our network of centre-left politicians, policy experts and academics from Europe and across the world to bring together ideas for a common approach around a new inclusive growth model for open societies. One that can combine innovation and dynamism with greater social justice, and equip their economies for the 21st century.

We would like to thank the Swedish Social Democratic party and the office of Swedish prime minister Stefan Löfven for their great support partnering with us to hold the Progressive Governance Conference in Stockholm in May 2016.

We would also like to convey our thanks to David Sainsbury, Center for American Progress, Fondation Jean-Jaurès, Friedrich-Ebert-Stiftung, Social Democratic party of Germany, and the offices of French prime minister Manuel Valls and German vice-chancellor

Sigmar Gabriel for the partnership that facilitated high-level seminars, in April 2015 and October 2015, of key policymakers and experts in Berlin and Paris. Those meetings laid the foundation of this volume and initiated an intellectual process which others have joined. In addition to the book's contributors we are extremely grateful to Michael McTernan, former director of Policy Network, for his inspiration and intellectual input to bring this volume together. Our thanks also go to Peter Mandelson, president of Policy Network, whose outstanding efforts in chairing and facilitating the Berlin and Paris seminars have helped to strengthen crucial ties and relations across our network and the centre left in Europe. We are grateful to Emma Kinloch and Katherine Roberts, who played a crucial role facilitating the seminars.

Thanks also to Renaud Thillaye, Ben Dilks and Simon Renwick for their invaluable assistance throughout.

ABOUT THE CONTRIBUTORS

Lodewijk Asscher is deputy prime minister of the Netherlands and minister for social affairs and employment. He also served, for several months in 2010, as acting mayor of Amsterdam.

Ed Balls is a senior fellow at the Mossavar-Rahmani Center for Business & Government at the Harvard Kennedy School and a visiting professor at King's College, London. He is a former UK shadow chancellor, secretary of state for children, schools and families, and chief economic adviser to the Treasury.

Thor Berger is an associate fellow of the Oxford Martin School at Oxford University, and a PhD candidate at the Department of Economic History at Lund University. Thor's work aims to understand how technological advances shape the growth of cities and regions from industrialisation until the present day.

Enrique Fernández-Macías is a research manager at Eurofound, Dublin. He holds a PhD in Economic Sociology from the University of Salamanca. His main research interests are job quality, occupational change and the division of labour.

Carlotta de Franceschi is co-founder and president of the Action Institute and former economic adviser to Italian prime minister Matteo Renzi. She previously spent 12 years in investment banking between New York and London (Credit Suisse, Morgan Stanley and Goldman Sachs) and holds an MBA from Harvard Business School.

Andrew Gamble is professor of Politics at the University of Sheffield and emeritus professor of Politics at the University of Cambridge. His most recent book is *Crisis Without End? The Unravelling of Western Prosperity.*

Pierre-Yves Geoffard is director of the Paris School of Economics. He has been a professor at the school since 2006 and his research interests include public economics, the economics of information and the microeconomic foundations of public health policies.

Peter A Hall is Krupp Foundation Professor of European Studies and a faculty associate of the Minda de Gunzburg Center for European Studies at Harvard University. He also serves as co-director of the Successful Societies Program, run for the Canadian Institute for Advanced Research. Peter is also a Centennial Professor in the European Institute at the London School of Economics.

Sara Hobolt is Sutherland Chair in European Institutions at the European Institute, London School of Economics and Political Science. She researches extensively on European Union politics.

Paul Hofheinz is president, executive director and co-founder of The Lisbon Council, a Brussels based thinktank dedicated to research on economic competitiveness and social renewal. Paul is an experienced editor and journalist, having worked as a writer and editor at *The Wall Street Journal.*

Karen Kornbluh is senior fellow for digital policy at the Council on Foreign Relations and a former US ambassador to the OECD.

She has also served as policy director for US president Barack Obama when he was in the Senate, and served the Clinton administration in a number of roles. Karen writes in a personal capacity.

Hannelore Kraft is premier of the German state of North Rhine-Westphalia. Hannelore is the first woman to hold the position of premier in the state since the creation of the post in 1946. Since 2009, she has been vice chair of the SPD and since 2007 the regional chair of NRW SPD.

Guillaume Liegey is a co-founder of Liegey Muller Pons (LMP), a campaign technology firm which advises progressive parties across Europe and beyond.

Silvia Merler is an affiliate fellow at Bruegel, a Brussels based thinktank. Silvia contributes to the research and policy analysis of the thinktank, with a particular focus on international and European macroeconomics. Previously, she has worked as an economic analyst at the European commission.

Dalia Mukhtar-Landgren is a senior lecturer at the Department of Political Science at Lund University.

Moira Nelson is an assistant professor at the Department of Political Science at Lund University. Her research focuses on examining determinants and consequences of social policy, and the vote-seeking incentives of governments to expand or retrench the welfare state.

Beth Simone Noveck is a former US deputy chief technology officer and director of the White House Open Government Initiative. She is a professor at New York University and the director and co-founder of The Governance Lab. She is the author of *Smart Citizens, Smarter State: The Technologies of Expertise and the Future of Governing.*

Frank Stauss is managing partner of the agency BUTTER, based in Düsseldorf, Berlin. His book *Höllenritt Wahlkampf* (Hell Ride Campaigning) was published in 2013.

Andrés Velasco is a professor of Professional Practice in International Development at the Columbia School of International and Public Affairs. From 2006 to 2010 he served as finance minister of Chile under President Michelle Bachelet.

Catherine de Vries is a professor of European Politics at the University of Oxford. Catherine is also a fellow of Lincoln College and an associate member of Nuffield College. She serves as the director of the Oxford Q-Step Centre.

INTRODUCTION

Once a vital source of future-facing visions and reforms, progressive movements today are struggling to convince voters and win elections. Between 2003 and 2015, centre-left parties have lost vote share in key European countries, including Denmark, Finland, Germany, Italy, Netherlands, Poland, Sweden and United Kingdom; in southern states, such as Greece, they face electoral decimation (see Figure I.1; see Sarah Hobolt and Catherine de Vries). Most notably, they are under pressure from all sides of the political spectrum – squeezed between new radical left forces, populist far-right parties, and a centre right that is determined to claim the centre ground.

Progressive parties must change, or risk dying. Survival in their current form seems less and less likely. Centre-left parties must define what they believe is a good society, adapting their structures and their policies to reflect a time when people have less trust in politics and state-centric solutions and technology is changing economies, societies and relationships.

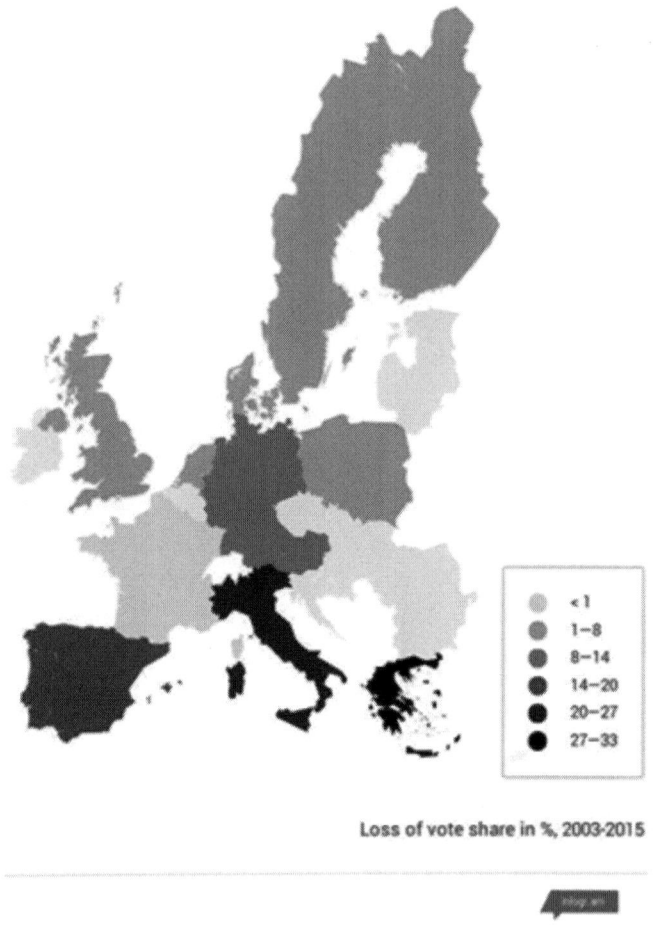

Loss of vote share in %, 2003-2015

Figure I.1   Europe's Progressives under Electoral Pressure.[1]

HOW THE FINANCIAL CRISIS WIPED OUT
THE LEGACY OF THE 2000s

One can argue that progressive parties' electoral deterioration is, among other factors, closely linked to two developments: the turn-of-the-century modernisation period and the centre left's inadequate response to the financial crash. The period of social democratic revisionism in the early 2000s was optimistic. At that time, centre-left leaders and thinkers successfully challenged the traditional view that deficit spending is the answer to low growth and unemployment. They maintained that individuals could be equipped for change through sustained investment in education, skills and active labour market policies; and they claimed that globalisation is, on balance, positive. Its gains could be harnessed internally and redistributed through investment in public services and innovative means of welfare spending.

However, the post-2008 consequences of the economic downturn – and crucially the interpretation of causes that led to the crisis – have greatly weakened the position of progressives. On the one hand, slow growth, low wages and a lack of trust in traditional elites has given rise to anti-globalisation movements and insurgents, with adverse consequences for both the centre left and centre right. On the other hand, the centre right succeeded in framing the cause of the financial crisis as public debt, responsibility for which has been pinned on the centre left.

The tacit public acceptance of the need for fiscal retrenchment has also meant that the centre left finds itself in an ambiguous position: when in power, in most cases, it embraces retrenchment, but in opposition, and at European level, it advocates Keynesian stimulus. This ambiguity has had damaging consequences for the social democratic brand. People fear that if progressives are in government they will act as 'tax and spenders' rather than reformers, which puts them in an electorally difficult position. The centre left's ambiguity about fiscal responsibility has left it open to attack by the centre right and an untrusting public. Because once in government the task has usually been to redefine fiscal policy "in a way that is progressive and economically sound" (see Andrés Velasco).

Although it also presents formidable challenges, the accelerating digital transition could prove to be progressives' salvation. It offers a promising reform agenda that could unleash economic growth and opportunities for some, but will only benefit all, in the long term, if progressives can move beyond social policies that were designed for the industrial age (see Karen Kornbluh).

POLITICAL ECONOMY IN TIMES OF TECHNOLOGICAL CHANGE

Developments in information and communication technology (ICT) are arguably producing a 'fourth' industrial revolution,[2] driven by innovations in artificial intelligence, big data, industrial robotics and an 'internet of things'. For policymakers and workers, the digital economy offers great opportunities – the chance for entrepreneurs to develop new, efficient and innovative businesses creating jobs, economic growth and high returns on investment – but especially for unskilled workers in traditional industries it offers high risks, placing huge strains on existing social security systems. Yet it also presents an opportunity for centre-left revival as it is commonly progressives who believe that "the future is a challenge to be embraced and not a curse to be avoided" (see Paul Hofheinz).

Europe continues to lag behind other parts of the world in productivity growth and innovation, especially in the service sector and ICT use.[3] Productivity is a key factor for boosting economic growth and increasing wages. Along with other key economic factors it varies greatly across the continent, representing a growing socioeconomic and political divide within countries and between north and south (see Silvia Merler). It is therefore vital that a distinctive progressive approach to innovation embraces the power and promise of innovation, but manages the societal impact.

The dark sides of globalisation must be seen in this context (see Ed Balls). There has been limited ability to redistribute the benefits of globalisation through state taxation. Tax evasion and in some cases powerful monopolies have grown, and efforts to shore up global governance to prevent arbitrage between national authorities have fallen short. If progressives cannot demonstrate that they will make globalisation work for inclusive and sustainable growth, there is a real danger of anti-growth and anti-trade populist sentiment spreading through the electorate. More than half of the population in advanced economies now see 'inequality' as a very big problem and 'growth' as only benefiting elites, whereas a decade and more ago they were more likely to see growth as a tide capable of 'lifting all boats'.[4] In addition, just as populists have made significant gains in recent years by playing on fears arising from globalisation, they may soon focus their fire on fears arising from digitalisation. Fear of the impact of technological change on jobs and privacy is leading some on the left to take uncompromising positions on global integration and trade but "at a time of widespread anxiety it is the responsibility of progressive leaders to promote a message of hope over fear" (see Frank Stauss).

If the left is to harness the energy and the opportunities of the digital and innovation economy, it needs to drastically upgrade its policy offer and be radical again in its approach to transforming the state. Such efforts include new thinking on how data and technology drive citizen engagement (see Beth Simone Noveck), a reform agenda that attracts finances for the economic recovery (see Carlotta de Franceschi) or the promotion of skills relevant to hi-tech jobs in a digital economy (see Thor Berger).

LABOUR, SKILLS AND EDUCATION IN THE DIGITAL ECONOMY

A generation ago, social democrats hoped and believed that the knowledge economy would increase demand for skills and higher levels of human capital. However, the reality is that there is greater evidence of labour market polarisation and heightened tensions and distributional conflicts between 'outsiders' and 'insiders' – those with stable jobs and solid career prospects, and those in more precarious employment or without a job altogether.[5] Embracing the innovation economy is crucial for progressive politics but the risk remains that in its current form it is not benefitting a wide segment of society.[6] In a great number of developed economies, among them France, Germany, Italy, Spain, the UK and the US, income inequality has substantially increased in recent years reaching unprecedented heights. At the same time evidence suggests that share of labour, the contribution of workers to gross value added, has gone down between four and 10 per cent from 1970 to 2014.[7] In combination with weakened labour regulations and global competition, technological advancements could widen the gap between poor and rich even further. In modern societies progressives should ensure workers reap the benefits of technology and robotisation while ensuring that opportunity is open to all (see Lodewijk Asscher). They might also put stronger emphasis on labour market institutions that follow the high-road model of Nordic economies rather than further flexibilisation (see Enrique Fernández-Macías).

The returns on talent in certain sectors are increasingly high, but, more generally, returns on productivity have remained low since the financial crisis. At the same time, the middle class feels increasingly threatened. Technological and communications developments, alongside emerging economies moving up the value chain, mean that global competition is stiffening. Once protected middle-class professions such as teaching, life sciences, engineering and accountancy, although still relatively well-paid, are witnessing a decline in wage premiums over time.[8] The digital economy seems to create business models that eliminate the need for middle-management and middle-income jobs, a development known as 'broken career ladders' that kicked off in the 'new economy' of the 1990s.[9] However, progressives should make a strong case for technology and innovation but foster it with training and social protections (see Pierre-Yves Geoffard).

The challenge for the centre left is to articulate a credible strategy that accommodates greater risk-taking and accepts economic and technological disruption while offering policies that create social cohesion, stability and security. This has to be at the heart of a forward-looking centre-left vision: one rooted in the future of work rather than the future of the welfare state. Rethinking the politics of social investment (see Hannelore Kraft) and what a solid net of universal social rights and guarantees could look like for unstable careers, abrupt changes in income, increased mobility across regions and countries and individualised life trajectories (see Peter A Hall). It might also mean looking at digital technology as a powerful tool for people to manage their own careers, set up their own businesses or get together with other 'atypical' workers to defend their rights in a more bottom-up fashion (cf ongoing transformation of the trade union movement). Yet, despite a set of new challenges the centre left must continue its pursuit of creating gender balance and guarantee better female labour market participation (see Moira Nelson and Dalia Mukhtar-Landgren).

MODERNISING PROGRESSIVE POLITICS

The challenges of building new coalitions in a 'high-risk, high-opportunity' era come as traditional parties are losing ground to social movements with distinctive insurgent styles and cultures of communication. Many mainstream parties are locked in 20th century thinking attached to traditional models of political organisation and communication while the world and the public have moved on. If social democrats are to argue for open societies, embrace digital platforms while advocating transparency and 'creative destruction', they also need to apply these principles to their own movements.

Social democratic parties have to reconsider the way they are constituted: their organisational form, internal politics and civic culture. Changing established institutions requires long-term pressure as resistance to reform within them is high, potentially rocking foundations and questioning people's authority and power. As a number of political scientists – from Francis Fukuyama[10] to David Runciman[11] – have observed, failure to change ultimately risks threatening the very existence of institutions. This is true for political parties, national governments as well as the EU today. There has to be zero tolerance of behind-doors favouritism or sectarianism. Progressives have to become "creative communities with a cause".[12] There is also a need to build on the practice of open primaries in France and Italy, learning from new social movements to choose candidates in more democratic and participative ways. Rightwing populism cannot be defeated with old style technocratic machine politics. Instead, progressives can reform and reinvigorate their movements by drawing crucial lessons from the way startups have built highly successful and innovative business models (see Guillaume Liegey).

Change, not defending the status quo, lies at the heart of any progressive policy agenda. The need for change is ever more apparent as we are living in an age of heightened risk regarding citizen's economic and physical security. At the same time there are many new opportunities: centre-left parties must resist being harbingers of doom. Some of the practical reforms suggested in this volume can help close the gap between risk and opportunity. For the last two decades social democrats have focused on education policy as a way of making globalisation and technological change more inclusive.

There have been many successes, but at the same time a feeling that current education policies are not sufficient to reverse the rising tide of inequalities. The 2016 Progressive Governance Conference (PGC) is therefore a chance to take stock: to assess where strategies of education reform have worked in realising progressive goals, and where the centre left can do better. The purpose of PGC 2016 is to forge a new agenda of progressive educational reforms: from early childhood education, to schools, to universities and technical vocational education that can prepare and empower our citizens for the challenges of the next decade and beyond. With education at its heart this conference takes forward the essays presented here on a more dynamic, skill-based and digital economy and the question of how progressives can strike the right balance between risk and opportunity.

NOTES

1. Figure was compiled using data from Global Elections Database, available from http://www.globalelectionsdatabase.com/, last access: 17.03.2016. No data for countries in light grey.

2. World Economic Forum (2016) *The Future of Jobs Employment, Skills and Workforce Strategy for the Fourth Industrial Revolution*, Cologny/Geneva.

3. Atkinson, R. D., McTernan, M. & Reed, A. (2015) *Sharing in the Success of the Digital Economy: A Progressive Approach to Radical Innovation*, London: Rowman & Littlefield International.

4. PEW Research Center (2014) *Emerging and developing economies much more optimistic than rich countries about the future: Education, hard work considered keys to success, but inequality still a challenge*, available from http://www.pewglobal.org/2014/10/09/emerging-and-developing-economies-much-more-optimistic-than-rich-countries-about-the-future/, last access: 23.07.2016.

5. Ranft, F. & Thillaye, R. (2015) 'Rapidly changing labour markets: is EU flexicurity still the answer?', in: Reuter, C [Ed.] *Progressive Structural Reforms. Proposals for European Reforms to Reduce Inequalities and Promote Jobs, Growth and Social Investment*, Brussels: SOLIDAR.

6. Driver, C. & Muñoz-Bugarín, J. (2010) 'Capital investment and unemployment in Europe: Neutrality or not?', *Journal of Macroeconomics*, Vol. 32, pp. 492–96; also: Organisation for Economic Co-operation and Development [OECD] (2011) *Employment Outlook*, Paris: OECD.

7. International Labour Organization et al. (2015) *Income inequality and labour income share in G20 countries: Trends, impacts and causes*, available from http://g20.org.tr/wp-content/uploads/2015/11/Income-Inequality-and-Labour-Income-Share-in-G20-Countries.pdf, last access: 18.03.2016.

8. Susskind, R. & Susskind, D. (2015) *The Future of the Professions: How Technology Will Transform the Work of Human Experts*, Oxford: Oxford University Press.

9. Osterman, P. (1996) *Broken Ladders: Managerial Careers in the New Economy*, Oxford: Oxford University Press.

10. Fukuyama, F. (2015) *Political Order and Political Decay: From the Industrial Revolution to the Globalisation of Democracy*, London: Profile Books.

11. Runciman, D. (2014) *The Confidence Trap: A History of Democracy in Crisis from World War I to the Present*, Princeton: Princeton University Trap.

12. Taylor, M. (2014) *Creative communities with a cause*, available from https://www.thersa.org/discover/publications-and-articles/matthew-taylor-blog/2014/04/creative-communities-with-a-cause/, last access: 17.03.2016.

Part I

Big Picture: On 21st Century Realities

REBUILDING ECONOMIC AND POLITICAL CAPITAL FOR EU INTEGRATION

Silvia Merler

Europe has been divided for much of its history, until the creation of the European Union introduced a 'new' peaceful and cooperating reality. In 2012, the EU was awarded the Nobel Peace Prize "for over six decades [having] contributed to the advancement of peace and reconciliation, democracy and human rights in Europe". The announcement came at a time when the hardship of navigating through the economic crisis was putting enormous strain on political cohesion within the EU. Today, as new challenges emerge, the EU appears to be more divided than ever since its creation. The divide is especially evident in the eurozone, where integration was the strongest before the crisis, and where economic, social and political divides persist today. At the broader EU level, strong centripetal forces were evident in the UK's urgency to renegotiate its 'status' within the EU and in the increasingly frequent tensions over the management of the refugee crisis. This contribution focuses on the eurozone, where the sharing of a single currency induces the deepest economic integration and imposes the need for the strongest political cohesion. It will look at the recent trends of Europeans' trust and satisfaction with the EU project and link them with the ongoing economic challenges, with the aim of highlighting relevant policy priorities.

THE FADING EUROPEAN POLITICAL CAPITAL

For a supranational union such as the EU, the trust of Europeans in EU institutions is an especially important metric of legitimacy. Data from the European commission's Eurobarometer survey shows that trust in the European institutions has been declining everywhere across eurozone member states since the beginning of the crisis, although more markedly so in those countries that have undergone adjustment programmes. In 2008 – before the outbreak of the global financial crisis – almost 75 per cent of respondents across Greece, Ireland, Portugal and Spain declared they tended to trust the European parliament, the European commission and the European Central Bank (ECB). By the end of 2013, the percentage had

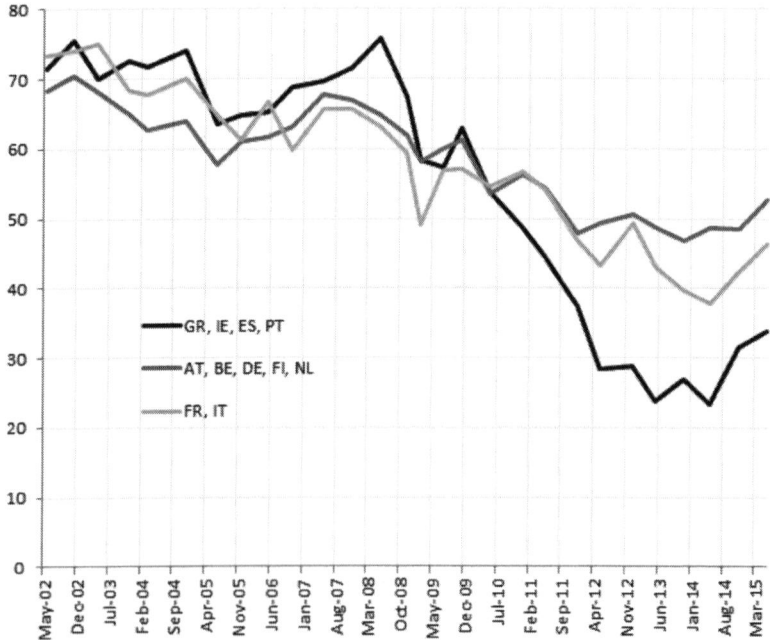

Figure 1.1   Percentage of Respondents Who Declare to Trust in EU Institutions.
Source: Author's calculations based on data from Eurobarometer; percentages are computed out of those who expressed a clear opinion ("don't know" answers are not counted). *Note*: Groups are constructed as averages weighted by population.

dropped to only 25 per cent on average across the same countries. Figure 1.1 suggests that trust levels in EU institutions bounced back in 2014 and 2015 in the programme countries, as well as in France and Italy (where it had declined but less markedly). Across those countries on which the impact of the eurozone crisis was less traumatic – ie Austria, Belgium, Germany, Finland and the Netherlands – trust in EU institutions decreased between 2008 and 2011 and has remained flat since then (see Figure 1.1).

Trust in national institutions appears to have been historically lower than trust in European institutions, with only 55–60 per cent of respondents declaring trust at the pre-crisis peak in 2007. Since then, things have evolved very differently across Europe. National institutions have lost sizable amount of trust in programme countries as well as in France and Italy, whereas they have gained in trust

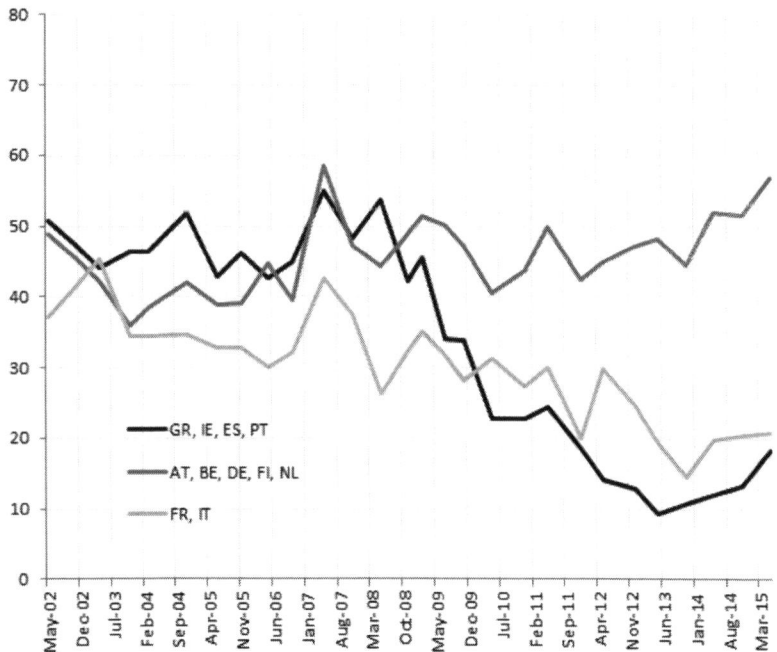

Figure 1.2 Percentage of Respondents Who Declare to Trust in National Institutions. *Source*: Author's calculations based on Eurobarometer data.

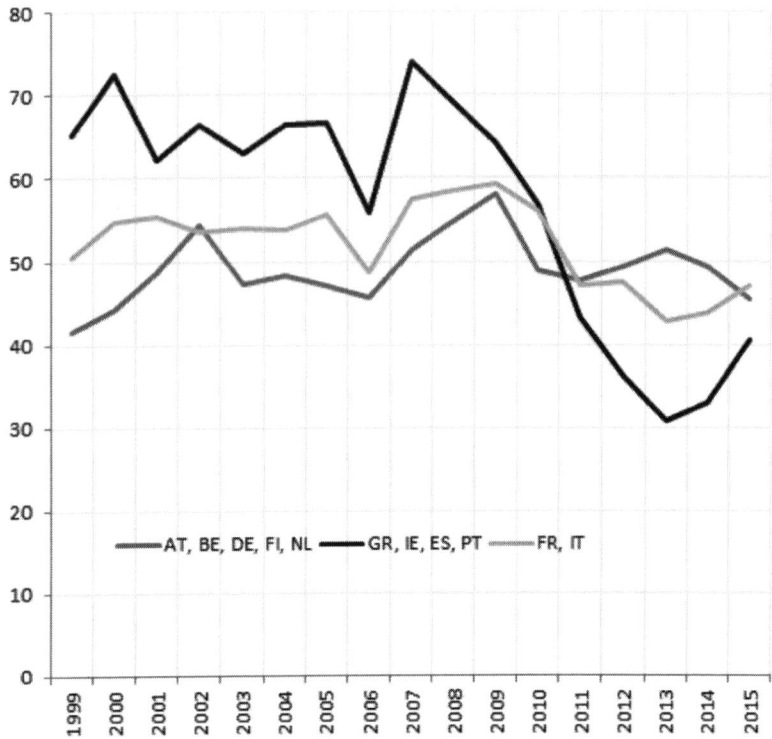

Figure 1.3 Percentage of Respondents Who Declare to Be Satisfied with Democracy in the EU. *Source*: Author's calculations based on Eurobarometer data.

compared to EU institutions across those countries that were less severely affected by the crisis (see Figure 1.2).

Particularly worrisome for a union that holds democracy among its core founding values, Europeans appear very dissatisfied with the way democracy works in the EU and in their own countries. The percentage of Eurobarometer respondents declaring to be "very satisfied" or "fairly satisfied" with "democracy in the EU" dropped from 75 per cent in 2007 to 30 per cent in 2013 across those countries that underwent macroeconomic adjustment programmes. Satisfaction with democracy in citizens' home countries has been in free fall since 2007, dropping from 70 per cent to 25 per cent in 2013. The latest data suggests a rebound in satisfaction with democracy at both the EU and country level, but the rebound is from a very low level and it might still be fragile (Figure 1.3).

THE ECONOMIC AND SOCIAL ROOTS OF THE DIVIDE

Europeans' evident distrust and dissatisfaction with the EU is strongly grounded in the economic crisis and its sizable social impact. The crisis brought back unemployment levels that had not been seen for a very long time. The unemployment rate for the Eurozone as a whole grew from 7.5 per cent in 2007 to 12 per cent in 2013, but the increase was very unbalanced across countries, with the figure reaching as high as 26–27 per cent in Greece and Spain. Moreover, unemployment hit the young generations especially hard. Across Greece, Ireland, Spain and Portugal, youth unemployment rates reached as high as 50 per cent on average in 2013 (Figure 1.4).

In the programme countries, as well as in France and Italy, youth unemployment has not only increased, but it has also become more persistent. The percentage of those who have been unemployed for longer than one year has increased considerably, and the entire distribution has shifted towards longer unemployment periods. In 2007 those who had been unemployed for longer than one year constituted less than 20 per cent of the total unemployed on average across the programme countries, whereas in 2014 they accounted for 42 per cent. A similar (although less sizable) increase is also found in France and Italy, whereas it is not common across countries in the so-called 'north' of the eurozone.

Prolonged youth unemployment can have very serious consequences. The longer young people stay out of the labour market, the more their skills deteriorate and become obsolete, making it more difficult to be re-employed. The increasing duration of youth unemployment is thus especially worrying, as it points to the risk that with unchanged policies some countries could be facing a future

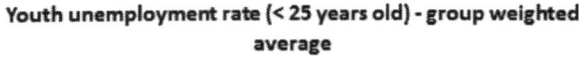

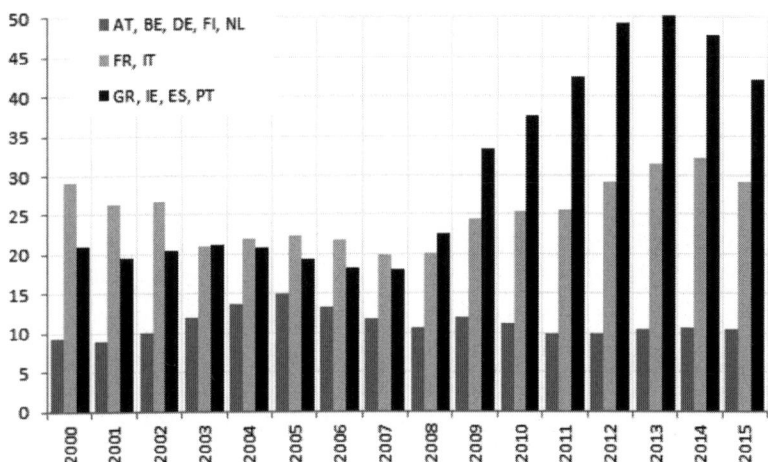

Figure 1.4 Youth Unemployment Rates. *Source:* Author's calculation based on Eurostat data.

of structurally higher unemployment. Faced with few opportunities at home, many people are leaving those countries that have been hit harder by the crisis: an analysis of the index of brain drain computed by the World Economic Forum in their Global Competitiveness Reports[1] shows that those countries that have been hit harder by the crisis have become less able to attract or even retain talent.

The economic crisis affected Europeans' distrust in the EU through its sizable social repercussions, which appear to have radically changed the *meaning* of the EU in the eyes of Europeans. The Eurobarometer survey also asks people what the EU means to them personally, and reports the percentage of people mentioning in their answers selected words such as "economic prosperity", "democracy", "unemployment" or "bureaucracy". Between 2008 and 2014, the percentage of respondents for whom the EU appears to be associated with the idea "unemployment" has increased while the percentage of people who associate the EU with the idea of "economic prosperity" and "democracy" has declined steadily across the programme countries as well as in Italy and France.

POLICY PRIORITIES

Europeans' distrust of EU institutions is a major threat to EU integration. While trust has shown sign of improvement recently, this rebound may be still too fragile to justify complacency. For trust to be solidly rebuilt, policy changes should aim at addressing the underlying social and economic roots of this discontent, in the attempt to rebuild a positive meaning for the EU in the eyes of Europeans.

Restarting growth requires financing for the real economy, which was severely reduced during the crisis. Banks in the countries that came under market stress tightened their lending to firms, with serious pro-cyclical consequences for those countries where firms' financing remains mostly bank-based. The effect was amplified by the fact that SMEs – the hardest-hit by the credit crunch – constitute a large share of the non-financial corporate sector in several eurozone countries. Banks have slowly restarted to lend to the real economy, but the credit recovery is uneven across countries. In this context, it is essential to broaden and diversify the financing opportunity of European firms. This will not only help in terms of financing the recovery but it will also enhance the resilience of the eurozone corporate sector to potential future crises, by fostering diversification in firms' funding sources. The project of a capital markets union, put forward by the European commission in September 2015, aims at achieving this objective. However, implementation to date has not been sufficiently ambitious and major obstacles to the integration of capital markets – including divergent accounting enforcement regimes, fragmented market infrastructure, or incompatible frameworks for the taxation of financial investment – remain untouched.[2]

Productivity is the cornerstone of economic growth. According to data from the Conference Board, the level of eurozone labour productivity is about 75 per cent of the US one when measured in terms of employment and 85 per cent when measured in terms of hours worked. Labour productivity growth in the eurozone has been positive after the crisis but yearly growth is below one per cent.

After the substantial contraction in total factor productivity (TFP) growth during 2008 and 2009, the eurozone had a positive TFP growth only in 2010 and 2011. The growth rate of TFP has been around zero in 2014, after two years of negative growth. It should be noted that significant variation exists in productivity across the eurozone, but improving productivity growth appears key to ensure sustainable growth.

Fostering productivity growth requires ultimately an understanding that competitiveness is essentially a firm-level phenomenon[3] and that looking at the aggregate average picture could be misleading and ineffective. An OECD[4] study comparing the contribution of firms to employment growth across 18 (mostly EU) countries over a 10-year period found that a small cohort of young and high-growth firms are net job creators and are responsible for a large proportion of employment growth.[5] Internationalisation and innovation are frequently considered to be very important drivers of productivity (at the firm level) and growth: the literature finds a strong relationship between internationalisation and innovation, suggesting that trade and innovation policies should be coordinated and integrated under a single responsibility,[6] so that policymakers would internalise the external effects of the individual policies.

Innovation plays a crucial role in fostering productivity and growth, but it requires investment. Based on a linear trend from 1970 to 2005, EU investment is currently estimated to be around €280bn below the pre-crisis/pre-boom trend (€170bn for non-construction investment), leaving little doubt about the urgency to act on this front. In particular, the crisis has widened the research and innovation divide in Europe[7]: innovation-lagging and fiscally weak countries in the EU cut their public research and innovation budgets during the crisis, while innovation-leading and fiscally stronger countries forged ahead with public R&I spending. In November 2014, the European commission headed by Jean-Claude Juncker announced an investment plan for Europe, aimed at mobilising at least €300bn in additional investment over the following three years via the creation of a European Fund for Strategic Investments.

The effect of this initiative remains to be assessed, but if it were successful in the objective of funding good projects that would not get financing otherwise, this could be an important turning point. The eurozone desperately needs solid growth to reduce unemployment levels across its member states and rebuild a positive meaning for European integration in the eyes of Europeans. Growth in turn is best achieved by "a policy mix that combines monetary, fiscal and structural measures at the union level and at the national level", as expressed by the ECB's president Mario Draghi in 2014.[8] Since then, the ECB has indeed embarked on unprecedentedly expansionary monetary policy, and this should be seized as a precious window of opportunity for pushing forward progressive structural and resolute actions.

At the same time, it is clear that rebuilding a positive meaning for the EU in the eyes of Europeans also requires addressing the evident dissatisfaction with the way democracy works in the EU (mentioned above). As I discussed in previous work on this issue,[9] the European parliament is the most trusted across European institutions, and in most of the countries it is more trusted than national parliaments. This is an important fact to keep in mind when discussing ways and means to bridge the actual and perceived democratic deficit in Europe. The idea that in order to provide for a stronger degree of legitimacy to European policies, national parliaments should be involved more does not sit well with the fact that citizens do not actually trust them any more – in reality, on average, way less – than the European parliament. Reinforcing the role of the European parliament, in turn, would possibly be an important step on the way to rebuilding trust in European institutions.

NOTES

1. World Economic Forum (2015) *The Global Competitiveness Report 2015–2016*, http://reports.weforum.org/global-competitiveness-report-2015-2016/.

2. Véron, N. (2015) 'Europe's Capital Markets Union and the new single market challenge', *Bruegel*, http://bruegel.org/2015/09/europes-capital-markets-union-and-the-new-single-market-challenge/.

3. Altomonte, C. & Aquilante, T. (2014) 'The 'dos and don'ts' of a growth-friendly policy mix for the Euro area', *Bruegel*, http://bruegel.org/2014/10/the-dos-and-donts-of-a-growth-friendly-policy-mix-for-the-euro-area/.

4. Criscuolo, C., Gal, P. N. & Menon, C. (2014) 'The dynamics of employment growth: New evidence from 18 countries', *OECD*, http://www.oecd-ilibrary.org/science-and-technology/the-dynamics-of-employment-growth_5jz417hj6hg6-en.

5. Aubrey, T., Thillaye, R. & Reed, A. (2015) *Supporting Investors and Growth Firms*, London: Rowman & Littlefield International, http://www.policy-network.net/publications/4916/Supporting-Investors-and-Growth-Firms.

6. Altomonte, C., Aquilante, T. Békés, G. & Ottaviano, G. (2014) 'Internationalism and innovation of firms', *Bruegel*, http://bruegel.org/2014/03/internationalisation-and-innovation-of-firms/.

7. Veugelers, R. (2014) 'Undercutting the future? European research spending in times of fiscal consolidation', *Bruegel*, http://bruegel.org/2014/06/undercutting-the-future-european-research-spending-in-times-of-fiscal-consolidation/.

8. Draghi, M. (2014) 'Unemployment in the euro area: Speech by Mario Draghi, 22 August 2014', http://www.ecb.europa.eu/press/key/date/2014/html/sp140822.en.html.

9. Merler, S. (2014) 'Is there a path to political union?', *Bruegel*, http://bruegel.org/2014/08/is-there-a-path-to-political-union/.

THE FUTURE OF THE WELFARE STATE

Peter A Hall[1]

The world is always in flux, of course, but sometimes it changes so profoundly as to render us "immigrants in our own land" – in the phrase of Margaret Mead – living in a world our parents never knew. The past four decades have seen the diffusion of radically new technologies, processes of economic and cultural globalisation, and a shift toward employment in services transformative of people's lives. In 1975, the personal computer had not yet been invented, developing economies produced less than a third of the world's output, and more than a third of workers in the OECD were employed in manufacturing. Today, the average American spends 23 hours a week on the internet; developing economies account for more than half of global production; and barely a fifth of the OECD labour force works in manufacturing.

Socioeconomic change on this scale has been especially consequential for the social programmes of the welfare state. The welfare state was an invention of the postwar years that assumed its current form during the 1960s and 1970s. To its programmes, the citizens of the developed democracies owe much of their security from adversity, but the adequacy of existing welfare states has been called into question by several challenges facing them today.

THE CHALLENGES

The capacity of existing social programmes to provide economic security is being strained by shifts in occupational structure that follow from rapid technological change and more intense international competition. In the developed world, well-paid manufacturing jobs are moving overseas, hollowing out the middle class, as people with advanced skills move into higher paying occupations, while others without them are relegated to low-paid jobs in services.[2] As a result, the distribution of market incomes has become more unequal, a phenomenon exacerbated in some economies by the decline of trade unions and the rise of the financial sector. These developments challenge states in two important ways. First, they increase the pressure on governments to redistribute resources at a time when slow rates of growth and high levels of debt limit the resources available to them.[3] Second, to maintain national prosperity in this new knowledge economy, governments have to ensure that firms have access to technological advances and workers are equipped with sufficient skills to exploit those advances.

These are social as well as economic challenges. From an egalitarian perspective, governments face the task, not only of providing sufficient skills, but of ensuring those skills are distributed widely across the population. Otherwise, a large part of the workforce may be consigned to low-paid, precarious jobs. If they lack the skills necessary for finding meaningful employment in such an economy or the advantages of birth conducive to acquiring those skills, many people will be deprived of the fruits of a high-technology economy. Moreover, failure on this front could have long-term consequences for social stratification. As income inequality increases, rates of social mobility decline, closing off the social escalators that provide a veneer of meritocracy in democratic societies.[4]

There is also an intergenerational dimension to these problems. Young people are especially at risk. In many countries, high levels of youth unemployment are impeding the entry of a younger generation into the core workforce.[5] The absence of stable employment delays family formation and depresses the birth rate, which can be debilitating for societies already facing the prospect of lower rates of growth as the average age of their population rises. Thus, governments face the problem of how to avoid the development of a new underclass, permanently excluded from well-paid employment and from the forms of social engagement associated with it.[6] They confront the spectre of intergenerational inequality with which welfare states that currently spend three times as much on the retired than they do on families with children are ill-equipped to cope.[7]

The political challenges facing those who would like to reform contemporary welfare states are equally great. The Keynesian welfare state was constructed, in the three decades after World War II, out of a politics in which the political cleavage between social classes loomed large. In many respects, that welfare state reflected a class compromise, in which parties representing the organised working class accepted a managed capitalism in exchange for social programmes, while parties speaking for the owners and managers of capital agreed to pay for this social safety net in return for industrial peace.[8] But the class cleavage no longer dominates politics in the developed democracies. As postwar prosperity reduced class-based grievances and the shift of employment to services eroded the blue-collar working class, it has become more difficult for centre-left parties to identify and speak for a cohesive class interest.[9] Today, the advocates for new social programmes face the challenge of assembling support for them from a more fragmented electorate, cross-cut by cleavages rooted in social values, new skill sets and fears about globalisation.[10] Moreover, many must often do so in contexts where scepticism about what governments can accomplish has increased, in the wake of slower rates of economic growth and the growing prominence of neoliberal ideas.[11]

THE ROLES FOR PREDISTRIBUTION AND SOCIAL INVESTMENT

The traditional instruments of the welfare state remain important to social wellbeing. Two kinds of programmes have long supplied the bedrock of the welfare state. Based on contributions from employers or employees, supplemented by general tax revenues, social insurance programmes protect people against the loss of income and costs associated with unemployment, retirement, illness and other adverse life events. Alongside them, redistributive programmes alleviate the worst effects of poverty and reduce inequalities in disposable household income through the provision of social assistance, tax credits and other types of subsidies.

However, these programmes do not fully address the socioeconomic challenges of the contemporary era. For that purpose, two other instruments on which this volume focuses have much more potential. One is a set of measures associated with predistribution, so-called because they are designed to address social inequality at its roots, by evening out the distribution of incomes set by market forces, reducing discrimination in the workplace or society, and advancing the life chances of the underprivileged in ways that do not entail fiscal redistribution on the part of governments.[12] Falling under this rubric are steps to enhance the influence of trade unions in wage bargaining; regulations requiring companies to provide more generous pensions, health care or other public goods; and mandates for private sector organisations that improve access to education, among other measures.

In an era when public spending is inhibited by the existence of large entitlement programmes and overhanging debt, policies of predistribution can reduce social inequalities at relatively low cost to governments. Although policymakers have to be attentive to potentially negative side effects, policies such as these can offset the effects of rampant shareholder capitalism on the inclination of firms to provide public goods and restore some of the 'beneficial constraints' that encourage firms to move their production up the value chain, thereby providing better jobs.[13] Requiring companies to offer better pay and benefits encourages them to produce higher quality products based on innovation and investment in the skills of their labour force. Asking them to pay for the environmental costs of their operations encourages them to seek sustainable forms of production.

Thus, predistribution is conducive, not only to more egalitarian societies, but to more effective competition in the global economy. The second set of instruments serving such purposes are those associated with social investment.[14] The defining feature of such policies is their emphasis on improving the skills of the workforce, broadly construed to encompass people's capacities to contribute to society as well as the economy. These programmes often do involve the expenditure of public resources and may target the least advantaged; but, unlike traditional redistributive policies, they are designed to enhance the productive capacities of the nation rather than only to relieve poverty. Such programmes include efforts to improve the educational level of the population, steps to facilitate re-entry of the unemployed into jobs, and measures focused on early childhood development to ensure all children realise their inherent potential.

Social investment addresses the central challenges of the new knowledge economy, which are to ensure that people have the skills to secure good jobs in a system of production transformed by technological change and that no one is denied access to such skills or good jobs by virtue of the circumstances of birth. As the term indicates, effective policies of social investment pay social dividends over time in the form of higher rates of economic growth that flow from better use of all the human capacities available in a society.[15] Genuine social investment does not simply force people into work but equips them to be more productive and socially engaged. Thus, it speaks to the problem of ensuring that the younger generations can enjoy a life as good as, if not better than, that of their parents.

Of course, the boundaries between these four types of instruments are porous. Predistributive measures can promote social investment, and effective social investment often entails some redistribution, as Huber and Stephens observe in this volume. However, policies oriented to predistribution and social investment speak more directly to the socioeconomic dilemmas of the contemporary era than traditional programmes of social insurance and redistribution do. As such, they deserve a prominent place on the platforms of progressive political parties.

THE POLITICS OF SOCIAL INVESTMENT

For progressive political parties, however, the issue is not simply whether to espouse policies of predistribution and social investment but how to assemble electoral coalitions around such a platform. As I have noted, many face electorates more sceptical than they once were about the value of state intervention and fragmented into constituencies that are sometimes resistant to the broad egalitarian appeals of the past.

However, it may well be possible for social democrats and their progressive counterparts to assemble a viable coalition around these policies, not least because their principal rivals on the centre right are also in trouble. Centre-right parties now operate under at least three handicaps. First, in Europe, the traditional appeal of Christian Democracy is waning because organised religion no longer occupies the central role it once had in many households. Women who could once be counted on to support Christian Democratic parties now vote in larger numbers for their Social Democratic counterparts, and a corresponding gender gap favours the Democrats in the US. Second, the breakdown of longstanding electoral cleavages has also had consequences for mainstream parties on the centre right. They too face an electoral constituency that is fragmenting, as parties on the radical right draw votes away from them with appeals that combine an attachment to traditional values with calls for social protection, while classically-liberal parties attract members with more progressive social values and a commitment to free markets.[16]

Perhaps most important, the mainstream centre right lacks an effective policy response of its own to the socioeconomic problems of the contemporary era. The suggestion that more intensive use of market competition can resolve those problems, which has been a staple of centre-right platforms for three decades, has lost much of its credibility in the wake of the 2008–2009 global financial crisis. As rising levels of income inequality dampen the prospects for social mobility, the traditional promise that centre-right governments would provide equality of opportunity in lieu of more equal incomes has become less convincing.

Moreover, because they are generally hostile to further regulation and public spending, these parties are largely unprepared to make the investments in public goods required for prosperity in the context of the new knowledge economy. Thus, the centre left faces an important political opportunity.

What must social democratic parties do in order to take advantage of this opportunity? There are two sides to their task. From within a fragmented electorate, they must construct coalitions of interest that bring together groups who might not otherwise be natural allies but who benefit from policies of predistribution or social investment. Comparative political economy suggests that political coalitions are always built on shared interests, and many of these policies speak to the concerns of groups that might not normally be seen as political bedfellows. Programmes of early childhood development, for instance, can serve the interests of working women and of the firms that employ them. Measures designed to stabilise or enhance employee pensions can speak to the interests of workers and of segments of the financial sector.[17]

In order to appeal to wide swathes of the electorate, these parties also have to build a new vision of what social democracy offers in the contemporary era. Successful political visions have at least two dimensions. On the one hand, they have to make a credible case that the policies being advanced are economically efficient, in the sense that they will address the socioeconomic problems of the day. As the chapters in this book indicate, such a case can be made for policies of predistribution and social investment. On the other hand, powerful political visions also have a moral dimension, which is to say they speak to overarching issues about what the people of a nation owe one another and can legitimately ask in turn of their government. Social democrats can find the basis for such a vision in longstanding conceptions of fairness underpinning each nation's understanding of social justice, and refashion it to speak to the circumstances of a changing world. This is not an easy task: it entails capturing and reframing aspects of the zeitgeist that are often elusive. But that is ultimately the craft of politics.

The core of such a vision lies in recognising that income inequality is a social problem but not the only problem confronting developed democracies. The most pressing issue is how to cope with the contemporary transformation in the economic conditions underlying national success. In large measure, that transformation lies behind rising levels of inequality and makes the task of addressing it more challenging. As the chapters in this book note, the rise of a knowledge economy means that national success today depends especially heavily on a nation's capacity to generate and exploit technological advancement. Compounding that problem is the transition to services, marked by the growth of employment in occupations dedicated to the production of services and a corresponding decline in manufacturing employment.

In short, at the centre of a progressive platform for the 21st century must be the claim that social democratic parties are best-equipped to manage the socioeconomic transformation of the contemporary era. The core challenge is not to rectify the wrongs of the past but to construct the conditions for national success in the future. Everyone's prosperity is at stake, and among the keys to success are policies of social investment and predistribution. Of course, appeals of this sort are not entirely new. They resonate with Harold Wilson's call in 1964 to reforge Britain in the white heat of the scientific revolution. But the terms of the economic challenge have changed and it requires new kinds of policies.

Moreover, rising to this challenge also entails giving some attention to issues of equality. Amidst rapid technological change, national success depends on mobilising the full capacities of a nation's people. Without a well-educated workforce, a country's firms cannot engage in the high value-added production that delivers rising living standards. And securing an educated labour force is not simply a matter of providing access to better schools. Educational achievement is conditioned by the social circumstances of the family. Thus, effective skill formation entails enough redistribution to promote a genuine equality of opportunity.

Progressive parties should note, however, that socioeconomic change has not simply created economic challenges. It has also disrupted the set of shared understandings and institutional practices that govern people's relationships with others and with the organisations central to their lives. In this respect, socioeconomic change has disorganised what we might think of as the contemporary social contract.[18]

There are many dimensions to these understandings, but some of the most consequential bear on what people can expect from their employers and what a nation expects of the firms at the centre of its economy. On these dimensions, in particular, the contemporary social contract has come unstuck. Under the impetus of more intense competition from open global markets and the influence of neoliberal ideas, many firms have cut costs by eliminating employee benefits, such as defined-benefit pension plans, and sub-contracting tasks to enterprises that offer their workers little job security and few benefits. In the wake of new compensation schemes for senior managers tied to the value of a company's shares, firms have begun to prioritise the value of those shares over returns to other stakeholders such as employees or local communities.[19] Financial manoeuvres to increase share prices, based on buy-back schemes and higher dividends have also drained funds away from investment in research and development, thereby reducing the capacity of many firms to contribute to national innovation and economic growth over the long term. Corporate opposition to environmental policies, such as carbon taxes, have pushed the costs of their operations onto society at large, threatening the sustainability of the economy.

In many instances, these practices have called into question longstanding understandings about what companies owe their employees and communities and generated widespread unease, reflected in contemporary debates about corporate social responsibility.[20] Thus, socioeconomic change does not simply pose challenges for the state. By unsettling many kinds of social relationships, it has given rise to a diffuse social discontent rooted in uncertainty about the terms of the prevailing social contract.

In this context, policies of predistribution can be seen as integral components of an effort to establish a new social contract. Social wellbeing cannot depend entirely on the actions of states. It also turns on what other social organisations, including firms, medical providers and universities, contribute to society, and predistributive measures are meant to ensure that they live up to their responsibilities to the common good. Thus, the times call for a new debate about how to define the terms of the social contract, with a view to shaping the predistributive measures that emerge from it.

Conventional understandings about social relationships at the macro-level, among different segments of society, have also been called into question by contemporary developments and should figure in this debate. Especially important here are questions about what the affluent strata in society owe people who are less advantaged than themselves. This has been a central issue since the dawn of civilisation, and it has been deeply affected by the nostrums of the neoliberal era, which present markets as the most efficient means of allocating resources, thereby privileging mechanisms that render access to many kinds of goods and services dependent on income. In this context, the notion that everyone is entitled to a certain level of public services has waned, and the right to income has been tied more directly to work, much as it was amidst another technological revolution at the turn of the nineteenth century.[21]

Debates about such matters involve issues of social justice, and the contemporary conjuncture supplies social democrats with new arguments to bring to them. They can rely on the fact that most people want to live in a just society. But they can also observe that, in the contemporary context, securing a just society is integral to securing a prosperous society. Social investment in people at the bottom of the social ladder unleashes productive capacities that enhance everyone's prosperity. If working women receive little help, they will not have children, and in the face of a dwindling population societies will decline. If skill formation at the bottom of the income ladder is unsuccessful, countries will be locked into economic regimes oriented to low-wage labour and the kind of low value-added production on which a developed country cannot build a successful economic base.

In short, efforts to advance social justice need not be seen as steps taken in spite of their economic inefficiency, but as measures that increase the efficiency of the nation as a whole, delivering widespread economic fruits. Once again, this is not an entirely novel idea: Victorian social reformers operated under similar premises. But that viewpoint has languished during the neoliberal age and deserves to be revived in light of contemporary socioeconomic challenges.

CONCLUSION

In recent years, disillusionment with what states can accomplish has led thoughtful analysts across the political spectrum to turn away from public action and look for solutions to contemporary social problems in a revived civil society, more socially conscious enterprises, and new forms of cooperation at the local level.[22] They are not wrong to do so. As I have noted, social wellbeing cannot depend entirely on the state. Bottom-up concerted action can address many kinds of social problems.

However, states and societies stand in a symbiotic relationship with each other. In some cases, effective social cooperation is easier to secure if public regulations guarantee the commitments social actors make to each other; and addressing some kinds of socioeconomic problems requires resources on a scale that can only be assembled by the state. Before giving up on the welfare state as an outmoded structure of ossified social programmes administered by purely opportunistic politicians, then, we should think seriously about how those programmes can be reshaped to meet the distinctive challenges of our age. And, as the chapters in this book suggest, inventive schemes of social investment and predistribution have the potential to speak directly to those challenges.

Of course, they are not a magic bullet capable of curing all the ills of our era, and there are many open questions about how they should be designed and funded. We know more about the desirability of improving the skills of the workforce, for instance, than about just how to do so. Programmes oriented toward early childhood development vary in quality and need to be carefully designed if they are to be effective. Regulations designed to encourage high value-added production can have adverse side effects that must be addressed if they are to accomplish their objectives. In many instances, such programmes must be tailored to the distinctive needs of a particular nation.

Nevertheless, there is real promise in the kind of creative rethinking of the welfare state that the chapters in this volume represent. After several decades in which many countries have seen median incomes stagnate and employment become more precarious, neoliberalism has lost much of its lustre, and programmes of social investment and predistribution look like viable alternatives that can work. In tandem with other social innovations, they surely have a role to play in the future of the welfare state.

NOTES

1. This chapter was first published in *The Predistribution Agenda: Tackling Inequality and Supporting Sustainable Growth* (I.B. Tauris, 2015), edited by Claudia Chwalisz and Patrick Diamond.

2. Autor, D. & Dorn, D. (2013) 'The growth of low-skill service jobs and the polarization of the U.S. labor market', *American Economic Review*, 103, pp. 1553–97; Oesch, D. (2013) *Occupational Change in Europe*, Oxford: Oxford University Press.

3. Schäfer, A. & Streeck, W. [Eds.] (2013) *Politics in the Age of Austerity*, Oxford: Polity Press.

4. Corak, M. (2013) 'Income inequality, equality of opportunity and intergenerational mobility', *Journal of Economic Perspectives*, 27, pp. 70–102.

5. More than 15 per cent of youth between the ages of 17 and 29 in Europe are not in education, employment or training; see also: Vogel, J. (2002) 'European welfare regimes and the transition to adulthood:

A comparative and longitudinal perspective', *Social Indicators Research*, 59, pp. 275–99.

6. Putnam, R. D., Frederick, R. B. & Snellman, K. (2012) 'Growing class gaps in social connectedness among American youth', *White Paper of the Saguaro Seminar*, Harvard University.

7. Bradshaw, J. & Holmes, J. (2013) 'An analysis of equity in redistribution to the retired and children in recent decades in the OECD and UK', *Journal of Social Policy*, 42, pp. 39–56.

8. Offe, C. (1983) 'Competitive party democracy and the Keynesian welfare state: Factors of stability and disorganization', *Policy Sciences*, 15, pp. 225–46; Huber E. & Stephens, J. (2001) *Development and Crisis of the Welfare State*, Chicago: University of Chicago Press.

9. Hall, P. A. (2013) 'The political origins of our economic discontents: Contemporary adjustment problems in historical perspective', in: Kahler, M. & Lake, D. [Eds], *Politics in the New Hard Times*, Ithaca: Cornell University Press, pp. 129–49.

10. Kriesi, H. et al. (2012) *Political Conflict in Western Europe*, Cambridge: Cambridge University Press; Wren, A. [Ed.] (2013) *The Political Economy of the Service Transition*, Oxford: Oxford University Press.

11. Hall, P. A. & Lamont, M. [Eds.] (2013) *Social Resilience in the Neoliberal Era*, New York: Cambridge University Press.

12. Hacker, J. S. (2011) 'The foundations of middle class democracy', in: *Priorities for a New Political Economy: Memos to the Left*, London: Policy Network, pp. 33–38; Hall, P. A. & Taylor, R. C. R. (2009) 'Health, social relations and public policy', in: Hall, P. A. & Lamont, M. [Eds.] *Successful Societies*, New York: Cambridge University Press, pp. 82–103.

13. Gomory, R. & Sylla, R. (2013) 'The American corporation', *Daedalus*, 142, pp. 102–48; Streeck, W. (1992) *Social Institutions and Economic Performance*, Beverly Hills: Sage.

14. Hemerijck, A. (2013) *Changing Welfare States*, Oxford: Oxford University Press; Morel, N., Palier, B. & Palme, J. [Eds.] (2012) *Towards a Social Investment Welfare State?* Bristol: Policy Press.

15. Heckman, J. (2012) *Giving Kids a Fair Chance*, Cambridge, MA: MIT Press.

16. Bale, T. (2008) 'Turning round the telescope: Centre-right parties and immigration and integration policy in Europe', *European Journal of Public Policy*, 15, pp. 16–45; Gidron, N. (2014) 'The centre-right in times of crisis: Evidence from the Netherlands', *Paper presented to the American Political Science Association*, Washington DC, August 2014.

17. Gingrich J. & Ansell, B. (2015) 'The dynamics of social investment: Human capital, activation and care', in: Beramendi, P., Häusermann, S., Kitschelt, H. & Kriesi, H. [Eds.] *The Politics of Advanced Capitalism*, New York: Cambridge University Press.

18. See also Azmanova, A. (2012) 'Social justice and varieties of capitalism: An immanent critique', *New Political Economy*, 17, pp. 445–63.

19. Gorman & Sylla; Jung, J. & Dobbin, F. (2014) 'Finance and institutional investors', in: Knorr Cetina, K. & Prada, A. [Eds.] *The Oxford Handbook of the Sociology of Finance*, New York: Oxford University Press, pp. 52–74.

20. Streeck, W. (2009) *Re-Forming Capitalism*, Oxford: Oxford University Press; Aguinas, H. & Glavas, A. (2012) 'What we know and don't know about corporate social responsibility: A review and research agenda', *Journal of Management*, 38, pp. 932–68.

21. Polanyi, K. (1944) *The Great Transformation*, Boston: Beacon Press; Hall, P. A. (2015) 'Social policy-making for the long term', *PS: Political Science and Politics*, 48, pp. 289–91.

22. Lawton, Cf. K. Cooke, G. & Pearce, N. (2014) *The Condition of Britain: Strategies for Renewal*, London: Institute for Public Policy Research; Henderson, R. (2014) 'Business Beyond the Public Sphere', *Presentation*, Harvard Business School, 30 January 2014. Available at http://www.hbs.edu/faculty/conferences/2014-business-beyond-the-private-sphere/Documents/Business%20Beyond%20the%20Public%20Sphere%20Introduction%20Slides.pdf (accessed 23 March 2015).

THE RISE OF CHALLENGER PARTIES AND THE DECLINE OF THE EUROPEAN LEFT

Sara Hobolt and Catherine de Vries

European democracies are undergoing a transformation. The major parties of the left and the right that have dominated politics for decades are losing ground. Some even argue that the "age of party democracy" has passed.[1] There are many indications that established political parties are in decline, including falling electoral support and turnout, the rise of voter volatility and declining party membership and party identification. The nature of political competition is also changing: the socioeconomic cleavages that used to dominate party competition and party ties are becoming less relevant, and new salient issues have emerged, such as immigration and European integration.

These developments present a particular challenge to the parties of the centre left. On the one hand, they need to appeal to the centre ground and the growing middle class, presenting themselves as fiscally responsible and economically liberal, while still being socially progressive. On the other hand, they do not want to abandon their core constituencies, who often fear globalisation, Europeanisation and immigration. The steady decline in the electoral support for centre-left parties is illustrated in Figure 3.1, which plots the percentage vote share of the main social democratic parties in Austria, Denmark, France, Germany and the UK since 1979. On average, centre-left support has declined in these countries from 41 per cent

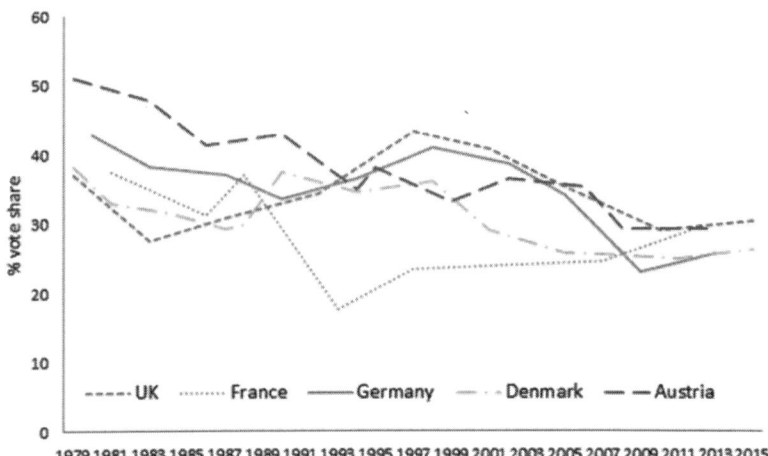

Figure 3.1   Decline of the Mainstream Left in Western European Countries.
Note: The percentage vote share of the main centre-left party.

in the early 1980s to 28 per cent today. In parallel to the decline of established political parties and an overall erosion of the 'old politics' of left and right, we are witnessing another trend, namely the rise of challenger parties.

To understand the plight of mainstream social democratic parties, it is important to examine the rise of another type of party, namely challenger parties. Challenger parties highlight issues such as European integration and immigration that have often been downplayed by the mainstream, and foster new linkages with voters that feel left behind by established parties. While the linkages between established parties and citizens are weakening as people are much less rooted in traditional civil society organisations such as unions, churches and the local community, challenger parties across western Europe give a clear voice to the discontent with the political establishment.

What distinguishes challenger parties from other 'mainstream' parties is that their primary goal is not to govern (officeseeking). Instead, they reshape the political landscape through their broad electoral appeal and ability to put new issues on the agenda. Notable

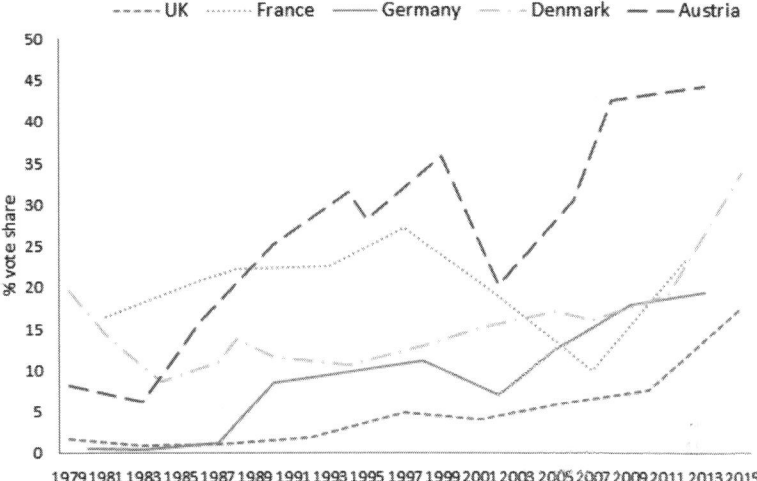

Figure 3.2   The Rise of Challenger Parties in Western European Countries. *Note: The percentage vote share of challenger parties.*

examples of successful challenger parties include Front National in France, the Freedom party in the Netherlands and Austria, Podemos in Spain, and the Five Star Movement in Italy. Such parties have transformed the nature of party competition and have restructured the political agenda, in most cases without ever setting foot in government.

In the recent Danish elections, for example, the Danish People's party became the largest party in the centre-right block with 21 per cent of the votes. Yet, despite offers to form a centre-right coalition government, they decided to stay in opposition, where they can gain influence on specific key policies (such as immigration), yet avoid the responsibility and accountability that comes with government.

Figure 3.2 illustrates the rise of electoral support for challenger parties in five western European countries, and shows a rapid increase in their support. Average support has increased from nine per cent to 23 per cent in just over three decades. While this is of a similar magnitude to the decline in the support for the centre-left parties over the same period, that is not to say that all voters of challenger parties are defectors from the mainstream left. However, it is noteworthy that while the most successful challenger parties are nominally located on the right of the political spectrum – eg the Front National in France, the Freedom party in Austria, the UK Independence party – they do attract significant support from dissatisfied social democratic voters. In Figure 3.2, the rise of challenger parties is mostly driven by populist rightwing parties, but not exclusively so. They also capture the rise of challenger parties on the left, such as the Red-Green Alliance in Denmark and Die Linke in Germany.

Clearly, the rise of challenger parties is influenced by broader societal developments,[2] but it is also driven by the degree to which political parties themselves are able to generate and maintain political demand. This rests on the assumption that politics is a competitive struggle among political parties about which political issues come to dominate the political agenda.[3] Parties are not vessels carrying societal divisions, but actively structure and determine the content of societal conflict. As a result, the substantive character of political competition will vary from election to election as new issues or positions are identified and mobilised by one party or another.[4]

Political parties politicise a previously non-salient event, policy issue, or societal conflict and attempt to increase public attention over this controversy. This logic is also at the heart of what Riker[5] coins as "heresthetics", which refers to a political strategy by which parties structure political competition in such a way that they gain leverage from competing on a preexisting dimension on which advantages are already held or by introducing an issue dimension that allows them to reshuffle the current structure of party competition to their advantage. The mainstream centre right and centre left have competed successfully on the economic cleavage and have dominated postwar European party systems.

Yet, in recent decades there has been a rise in the salience of 'new politics', including issues such as immigration and European integration, but also issues like law and order and defence.[6] Challenger parties play a key role in mobilising grievances on those issues that often cut across the traditional economic left-right dimensions. In this view, new parties emerge not only because a societal demand for them exists, but perhaps more importantly because these parties are able to actively shape and craft their own demand.

But who are these challenger parties? The literature suggests that challenger parties are those that do not occupy a winning position in the political system and thus have incentives to act as challengers to the mainstream. In the US context characterised by a majority government and competition among two parties, challenger parties are defined as parties in opposition. In the western European context of coalition government and a multitude of parties, challenger parties are less easily defined.

Muller and Strøm's[7] seminal work on party competition in the European context outline that party leaders value three goals: office, policy and vote. Yet, there are potential trade-offs among these. For example, established parties of the left responded to the decline of cleavagebased voting by shaking off some of their ideological origins and become more catch-all, such as the third-way social democrats in Britain, Germany or the Netherlands, in order to enhance their electoral appeal.[8] They thus have favoured votes and office over policy.

As the left-right ideological distance between social democrats and conservatives or Christian democrats began to shrink as a result,[9] it provided a strategic opportunity for challenger parties to gain a foothold in the system and put new issues on the agenda as the salience of the left-right divide was somewhat diminished.[10]

Challenger parties have responded to these developments by not being primarily office-seeking, as this would forge them into difficult concessions with mainstream competitors (a lesson painfully learned by challengers such as the Freedom party in Austria or the List Pim Fortuyn in the Netherlands in the mid-1990s and early 2000s).

Given that the existence and success of challenger parties is linked to the mobilisation of issue dimensions other than the left-right

government participation carries considerable risk. It requires difficult policy comprises, forces parties to moderate their positions and
stake out positions on a large set of issues. This is difficult for every
party, but especially for those that have distinctive issue pallets.

Rather than seeking office, challenger parties aim to reshape the
political landscape through their broad electoral appeal and ability
to put new issues on the agenda. Even if challenger parties do seek
office, they are often not willing to compromise on their core issue
positions. This is illustrated by recent events in Greece. Syriza did
not seek to enter a coalition with a centre-left party which was more
willing to accept austerity demands coming from Brussels, but rather
entered into a coalition with a radical right party with whom they differ on many respects but not on how to negotiate with EU creditors.
Indeed, there are many examples of successful challenger parties,
such as the Front National in France, the Freedom Party in the Netherlands, and the Danish People's party in Denmark, that have transformed the nature of party competition without being in government.

To attract voters challenger parties pursue both programmatic
strategies, relating to the importance they attach to issues and the
positions they take on these issues, and charismatic strategies that
stress the personality of the leader, an overall sense of opposition to
the ruling establishment and a reliance on emotional appeals.[11]

Programmatically, challenger parties mobilise issues previously
ignored by the mainstream, something we coin issue entrepreneurship, and adopt a variety of positions that cannot easily be sum-
marised in left-right terms, a strategy we refer to as issue flexibility.[12]
This does not only allow them to carve out a distinct ideological
appeal that is recognisable to voters,[13] but also to strategically drive
a wedge within platforms of established parties that partly ignored
issues like immigration or European integration in order not to spark
off intra-party dissent.[14] Issue entrepreneurship and issue flexibility
are the prerogative of challenger parties rather than established parties as the former are not constrained by historical legacies linked to
long-standing social divisions and therefore have much more room
for programmatic malleability.

Charismatically, challenger parties are explicitly anti-establishment, emphasise the personality of the leader and use emotional appeals in their rhetoric. This charismatic strategy allows challenger parties to carefully craft a basis of support amongst those voters that felt left behind by mainstream politics, for example lower-class voters in Britain to which the centrist positions of the Labour party do not appeal, or traditionally Christian Democratic and Conservative voters in the Netherlands who worry about internationalist stances of their parties.

What is crucial for the strategy of challenger parties and their success is the combination of programmatic and charismatic strategies. This combination allows challenger parties to make even distant and technocratic issues, like European integration, into a vote winner and allows them to merge a diverse set of issue positions into a coherent narrative about the failings of the establishment.

This conceptualisation of challenger parties as those who are not primarily office-seekers, but vote- and policy-seekers that use distinct programmatic and charismatic strategies to reshape the political landscape through their broad electoral appeal and ability to put new issues on the agenda, allows us to highlight commonalities between challengers on the left and the right that have so far been treated in isolation. Leftwing parties like Podemos in Spain and Syriza in Greece, although different in ideological outlook, in fact have many commonalities with rightwing parties like the Party for Freedom in the Netherlands or the UK Independence party when it comes to their programmatic and charismatic strategies. These parties also present a distinct challenge to the mainstream left as they often appeal to voters who are dissatisfied with the political class and who feel that the mainstream centre-left does not represent their interest. One group of voters attracted to challenger parties, and their opposition to 'politics as usual' are those voters who feel like the losers of globalisation: the less educated, lower skilled or the unemployed – among them many who would have traditionally been seen to be part of the mainstream left's natural constituency. Many of these voters support the parties based on their issue positions that differ from the mainstream, most notably Eurosceptic and anti-immigration stances, but also in support of a new and different kind of politics. Because challenger parties are mostly not part of government (coalitions) yet can draw on substantial electoral support, they are able to extract policy concessions from established parties to which they constitute a significant electoral threat – yet, without the 'cost of governance' associated with actual government responsibility. As a result, challenger parties are able to influence government policy without being part of government itself, which in turn allows them to regain and capitalise on their anti-establishment appeal.

NOTES

1. Eg: Mair, P. (1990) *The West European Party System*, New York: Oxford University Press; Dalton, R. J. & Wattenberg, M. P. [Eds.] (2000) *Parties without Partisans*, Oxford: Oxford University Press.

2. See, for example: Kriesi, H. et al. (2008) *West European Politics in the Age of Globalization*, Cambridge: Cambridge University Press.

3. Schattschneider, E. E. (1960) *The Semisovereign People: A Realist's View of Democracy in America*, New York: Holt, Rinehart & Winston.

4. Carmines, E. & Stimson, J. A. (1989) *Issue Evolution: Race and the Transformation of American Politics*, Ithaca: Princeton University Press; Riker, W. H. (1982) *Liberalism against Populism: A Confrontation between the Theory of Democracy and the Theory of Social Choice*, San Francisco: W.H. Freeman and Co.

5. Riker, W. H. (1996) *The Strategy of Rhetoric: Campaigning for the American Constitution*, New Haven: Yale University Press, pp. 9–10.

6. Kriesi, H. et al. (2008) *West European Politics in the Age of Globalization*, Cambridge: Cambridge University Press, pp. 59–60.

7. Strøm (1999).

8. Kirchheimer (1966); Kitschelt, H. (1997) 'European Party Systems: Continuity and Change', in: Rhodes, M., Heywood, P. & Wright, V. [Eds.] *Developments in West European Politics*, Macmillan.

9. Kitschelt, H. (1997) 'European Party Systems: Continuity and Change', in: Rhodes, M., Heywood, P. & Wright, V. [Eds.] *Developments in West European Politics*, Macmillan; Van Kersbergen (1997).

10. Adams, J., de Vries, C. E. & Leitner, D. (2012) 'Which Subconstituencies Reacted to Elite Polarization in the Netherlands? An Analysis of the Dutch Public's Policy Beliefs and Partisan Loyalities, 1986–1998', *British Journal of Political Science*, 42(1), pp. 81–105.

11. Kitschelt, H. (2000) 'Linkages between Citizens and Politicians in Democratic Polities', *Comparative Political Studies*, 33(6/7), pp. 845–79; Van der Brug and Mughan (2007).

12. Hobolt, S. & de Vries, C. E. (2015) 'Issue Entrepreneurship and Multiparty Competition Comparative Political Studies', 48, pp. 1159–85.

13. Meguid (2008).

14. de Vries, C. E. & Hobolt, S. B. (2012) 'When dimensions collide: The electoral success of issue entrepreneurs', *European Union Politics*, 13(2), pp. 246–68; Van de Wardt, M., de Vries, C. E. & Hobolt, S. B. (2014) 'Exploiting the cracks: Wedge Issues in Multiparty Competition', *Journal of Politics*, 76(4), pp. 986–99.

REFERENCES

Adams, James, Catherine E. de Vries, and Debra Leitner. 2012. Which Subconstituencies Reacted to Elite Polarization in the Netherlands? An Analysis of the Dutch Public's Policy Beliefs and Partisan Loyalities, 1986–1998. *British Journal of Political Science* 42(1): 81–105.

Carmines, Edward and James A. Stimson. 1989. *Issue Evolution: Race and the Transformation of American Politics*. Ithaca: Princeton University Press.

Carmines, Edward and James A. Stimson. 1993. On the Evolution of Political Issues. In *Agenda Formation*, ed. William H. Riker. Ann Arbor: University of Michigan Press, 151–68.

de Vries, Catherine E. and Sara B. Hobolt. 2012. When dimensions collide: The Electoral Success of Issue Entrepreneurs. *European Union Politics* 13(2): 246–68.

Dalton, Russell J. and Martin P. Wattenberg (eds.). 2000. *Parties without Partisans*. Oxford University Press.

Hobolt, Sara and Catherine E. de Vries. 2015. Issue Entrepreneurship and Multiparty Competition. *Comparative Political Studies*, 48(9): 1159–85.

Kitschelt, Herbert. 1997. European Party Systems: Continuity and Change. In M. Rhodes, P. Heywood and V. Wright (eds.). *Developments in West European Politics*. Macmillan.

Kitschelt, Herbert. 2000. Linkages between Citizens and Politicians in Democratic Polities. *Comparative Political Studies* 33(6/7): 845–79.

Kriesi, H., Edgar Grande, Romain Lachat, Martin Dolezal, Simon Bornschier, and Timotheos Frey. 2008. *West European Politics in the Age of Globalization*, Cambridge: Cambridge University Press.

Mair, Peter. 1990. *The West European Party System*. New York: Oxford University Press.

Muller, Wolfgang C. and Kaare Strøm (eds.). 1999. *Policy, Office, or Votes? How Political Parties in Western Europe Make Hard Decisions.* Cambridge: Cambridge University Press.

Riker, William H. 1982. *Liberalism against Populism: A Confrontation between the Theory of Democracy and the Theory of Social Choice.* San Francisco: W.H. Freeman and Co.

Riker, William H. 1996. *The Strategy of Rhetoric: Campaigning for the American Constitution.* New Haven: Yale University Press.

Schattschneider Elmer E. 1960. *The Semisovereign People: A Realist's View of Democracy in America.* New York: Holt, Rinehart & Winston.

Stimson, James A., Cyrille Thiébaut, and Vincent Tiberj. 2012. The Evolution of Policy Attitudes in France. *European Union Politics* 13(2): 269–80.

Van de Wardt, Marc, Catherine E. de Vries, and Sara B. Hobolt. 2014. Exploiting the Cracks: Wedge Issues in Multiparty Competition. *Journal of Politics* 76(4): 986–99.

BEYOND THE THIRD WAY: A NEW INCLUSIVE PROSPERITY FOR THE 21ST CENTURY

Ed Balls[1]

It is now almost 20 years ago that US president Bill Clinton and UK prime minister Tony Blair launched the progressive governance movement and called for a 'third way' in response to the challenge of globalisation.

Their purpose was to chart a course between passive, free-market laissez-faire on the one hand, and the rejection of open, global markets and a lurch to protectionism on the other. Their ambition was to show that a dynamic market economy and a fair society could go hand in hand.

Two decades on, this clearly remains work in progress.

Governments across the developed world continue to struggle with the consequences of seismic global and technological change, financial instability, rising inequality and stagnating median incomes.

And political disenchantment has continued to grow. Politicians of all parties, and in all countries, hear regularly on the doorstep the worries and fears of people that economic recovery is not working for them and their family. Not surprisingly, far-right and -left populist movements have flourished, as recent polls and political developments in both the US and UK amply demonstrate.

In the face of such powerful global changes, we cannot take public support for this open, global vision of a dynamic market economy for granted. So how should progressive politics respond?

THE THIRD WAY OF THE 1990s

My starting point is the economic trends we have seen over the last 20 years and what they teach us about how we should shape our economic policy for the next 20.

Looking back, there are important differences to today – but also some striking similarities too.

Back then, the UK was recovering from a deep recession, following the exchange rate mechanism crisis. The fiscal deficit was very large and household incomes were being squeezed by tax rises and cuts to public spending.

And the political debate was focussed on the big global economic changes taking place – the rapid growth of international trade; new competition in manufacturing from emerging economies in eastern Europe and Asia; and technology replacing jobs and undermining wages among low-skilled, manual workers.

Of course, this debate was taking place across the developed world.

In America, as debate raged about the North American Free Trade Area and newspaper columnists agonised over what they called 'the downsizing of corporate America', the first-term President Bill Clinton called a G7 jobs summit in Detroit.

In Britain, as we debated the case for Bank of England independence and new fiscal rules to prevent another ERM-style crisis, Tony Blair and Gordon Brown led the public debate about how Britain should respond to these economic changes by calling for a 'skills revolution'.

Meanwhile, Europe's response was a single currency to deliver stability, a single market to deliver rising prosperity and a social chapter to deliver fairness. All of this was much to the anguish of the Eurosceptics.

TWENTY YEARS ON

If a new insecurity was taking hold in the 1990s, today those concerns are deep, entrenched and undermining public trust that politics can offer a solution.

Indeed, the pattern we have seen in the UK – growth returning, but feelings of insecurity and discontent being expressed in the opinions polls – has been repeated in the US, France, Denmark and Austria too.

The best we can say is that the struggle to prove that a dynamic market economy and a fair society can go hand in hand remains to be won.

Some would say that the Blair-Clinton attempt to forge a third way did not succeed.

That steps were taken to improve the prospects of lower-paid workers, including higher national minimum wages and more generous tax credits to make work pay.

But not enough was done to improve the prospects of the non-university educated workforce. While the failure of financial regulation led to a global financial crisis and the global recession which followed hit middle- and lower-incomes families particularly hard.

I have some sympathy with this argument. In the UK, we did not do enough on skills and the failure of all parties in the UK, and all countries in the developed world, to see the coming crisis was a huge error.

But I do not believe that the progressives were wrong in their central belief that a path could be taken between free-market economics and protectionism and isolationism.

My argument is that the third way did not deliver because the world was changing in a more profound way than any of us anticipated.

And new times now demand a new approach.

Not only do we face new challenges from technological change and globalisation, we must also deliver at a time when both monetary and fiscal policy face great challenges.

So charting a new way forward for the even more challenging century we now live in is now the challenge for this generation – politicians, businesses, and trade unions – all of us.

THE 21st CENTURY ECONOMIC CHALLENGE

Over the last 20 years, the global economy has fundamentally changed – and changed for the better.

As communism collapsed and countries have liberalised their economies, there have been significant reductions in poverty and increases in living standards across Asia, south America, eastern Europe and now Africa.

Meanwhile, developments in information and communications technology have transformed the way we live our lives and brought the world ever closer together.

And as these trends have accelerated, the global economic map has been redrawn as new opportunities have opened up not just for developed countries, but for emerging markets like China and Brazil.

Back in the 1990s, we recognised that globalisation was creating new challenges. Trade and technology placed a premium on higher level skills and qualifications, and reduced low-skilled jobs.

Changes to the structure of labour markets – often caused by the strain of global competition and including the fall in trade union membership – also had a knock-on effect on wages.

And having more working mums has helped to increase living standards – but also made providing affordable childcare and family-friendly employment rights more important too.

While progressives attempted to address all of these challenges, we failed to foresee three other changes which were going to fundamentally reshape our world.

First, global economic integration led to much greater instability in our financial and tax systems than any of us anticipated.

As we now know, the global financial sector was taking risks that both bankers and regulators did not fully comprehend.

As leverage increased and balance sheets grew, bulging corporate tax receipts gave the impression that everything was rosy.

And in Britain, the Labour government ended self-regulation by introducing the Financial Service and Markets Act.

But while voices in the City and across the right argued that we were being too tough on the financial sector, we should have been much tougher still.

And when the global crash came, the result was the near-collapse of the financial system and unprecedented state intervention in our banking sector.

Alongside this, globalisation also created much greater complexity in our tax system. Offshore tax havens, transfer pricing arrangements and well-paid accountants have all helped some international firms stay one step ahead of the taxman, while technology companies, which do not need a shop front that physically anchors them in a particular country, have benefited in particular.

Second, labour mobility has also been much greater than anyone expected. Just as hundreds of thousands of eastern European people have come to live and work in the UK, so too have millions of Mexicans and Latin Americans moved to the United States, and Indians and Chinese to the relative riches of the Middle East – a new global and mobile middle class.

Additional competition for low-skilled jobs, and increasingly intermediate-skilled jobs, has put great pressure on communities. And developing countries' use of natural resources like energy, water, precious metals and other commodities has risen.

Third, we have seen profound technological change which is not just substituting for unskilled labour, but replacing traditional middle-income jobs too.

Two decades ago, we were right to worry that low-skilled jobs in sectors like manufacturing would go overseas. Sophisticated machine tools and software are already reducing the need for routine jobs on production lines and in offices. But the advances in robotics and artificial intelligence – 3D printers, not to mention Google's driverless cars or Amazon's drones – mean that intermediate skilled jobs are also being lost too, in what economists call a 'hollowing out' of the labour market.

Meanwhile at the top, the returns from ideas, capital and top-class qualifications are getting greater and greater. And the result has been, for most developed countries, rising income inequality on a scale not seen since before the first world war.

No developed country has escaped the impact of these global trends. All are dealing with the twin challenge of dealing with the aftermath of the financial crisis, while also trying to adapt to the relentless forces of globalisation, immigration, and technological change. But the UK has been particularly hit hard:

- Britain's financial sector – larger and more exposed to international shocks than our competitors – has experienced bigger hits to growth and to the fiscal position.
- The UK's openness and 'safe haven' reputation, alongside the lack of transitional controls on EU accession states in 2004, has seen low-skilled immigration put additional pressure on our labour market.
- And while many countries have tried to increase labour market flexibility in the face of 'hollowing out' the UK has seen a particular shift to low-wage, part-time and often insecure employment.

A NEW INCLUSIVE PROSPERITY FOR THE 21st CENTURY

So how do we respond? Some on both the left and right say that if rapid globalisation and technological change have undermined the pay and prospects of working people, then the simplest thing to do is to turn our back on those economic forces – putting up trade barriers, stopping migration into Britain and leaving the European Union.

In my view, Britain has always succeeded, and can only succeed in the future, as an open and internationalist and outward-facing trading nation, with enterprise, risk and innovation valued and rewarded, by backing entrepreneurs and wealth creation, generating the profits to finance investment and winning the confidence of investors from around the world.

Turning our face as a nation against the rest of the world and the opportunities of globalisation is the road to national impoverishment

Open markets and business investment are part of the solution, not the problem – as is a Britain that is properly engaged in a reformed Europe.

But we cannot just bury our heads in the sand and ignore the legitimate and mainstream concerns of people across our country that our economy is not currently working for them and their families.

A return to business as usual won't work. It won't work economically. There is no future for the UK in trying to compete on cost with emerging countries round the world.

It won't work politically either. Cutting workers' rights, undermining public services and reducing taxes only at the top in the hope that wealth will trickle down will not persuade a sceptical and hard-pressed electorate.

New times demand a new approach. And I want to set out three ways that I believe that a new inclusive prosperity for the 21st century must be different from the approach taken in the 1990s:

- First, we need tougher global co-operation.
- Second, we need good jobs and skills, especially for those being left behind.
- And third, we need a new industrial policy.

HARD-HEADED INTERNATIONALISM

First, we need a much tougher international response to these global trends. We have to show that we understand and can respond to people's concerns about financial instability, immigration and tax avoidance while staying open to the world and continuing our commitment to a dynamic market economy.

I call this a hard-headed internationalism – and it must start with Europe.

We know that we need reform of the EU to deliver value for money for taxpayers and to make Europe work in our national interest. But it is not in our national interest to walk away from the huge single market on our doorstep. To do so would be anti-investment, anti-jobs and anti-business.

Instead of marginalising ourselves with fringe parties, and isolating ourselves from key allies, we should be at the centre of the debates. And we need that cooperation to make progress in vital areas, including on security, trade and climate change.

On financial regulation, we need new impetus to global efforts to reform our financial system which are grinding to a halt.

On immigration, too, we need greater international cooperation so that we can keep the benefits of skilled migration, while controlling and managing it fairly – and finding a fair solution for refugees.

This means new laws to stop agencies and employers exploiting cheap migrant labour; while also making sure people who come to this country learn English and contribute to Britain. While in Europe, we need longer transitional controls, stronger employment protection and restrictions on benefits – because when we face such an acute challenge to make work pay for unskilled people, we should not be subsidising unskilled migration from the rest of the EU.

And on business taxation, we also need greater international cooperation to strike a fairer deal for the future. Our system must be competitive, promote long-term investment and innovation, and be simpler, predictable and fair. The purpose of a competitive tax system must be that companies view Britain as a great place to do business, not simply a cheap place to shift their profits.

So alongside action in the G20 and OECD to tackle tax avoidance and enhance transparency, we need a business tax system that promotes long-term investment, supports enterprise and innovation, provides a stable and predictable policy framework for business and a foundation built upon fairness. With this approach, Britain can compete in a race to the top, with a highly skilled, productive work-force directly benefiting from sustainable economic growth.

WORK AND SKILLS

The second task for our inclusive prosperity agenda is to provide good jobs and skills for everyone and especially for those who feel they have been left behind.

Demand for high-skilled jobs in advanced manufacturing, financial and business services, and across the creative industries will continue to increase – so we must maintain our global excellence in higher education.

But we must also ensure that the highest skills can be achieved through our vocational system. We cannot just meet the shortage in trained technicians that businesses repeatedly highlight by importing labour.

Those with intermediate skills are most at risk of the 'hollowing out' phenomenon. We must help equip them to take up new opportunities as baby boomers retire and ensure the skills they have developed are recognised by prospective employers.

In lower-skilled sectors, we must ensure that the minimum wage continues to increase, is properly enforced and that employers have clear incentives to pay a living wage – with tax credits an added reward for hard work rather than a subsidy for low pay, and training available to all to support career progression.

We must ensure that young people entering the world of work have the ambition, skills, knowledge and qualifications they will need to succeed.

We need a major expansion of university technical colleges to ensure Britain is producing enough trained technicians in Stem subjects and other subjects where there is clear demand.

We need to get young people into training rather than unemployment, and improve the quality of apprenticeships, with a greater role for employers in designing vocational qualifications and a key role in commissioning and planning skills provision in their area.

A NEW INDUSTRIAL POLICY

And third, to deliver inclusive prosperity, we need to match policies for open markets and skills with a new industrial policy which puts innovation, long-termism and growth centre stage.

After the debacle of British Leyland in the 1970s, 'industrial policy' were dirty words in Britain. So while Margaret Thatcher had an industrial policy in the 1980s – the Big Bang for financial services, bringing Japanese car manufacturers to Britain and investing heavily in Airbus and its supply chain, including Rolls-Royce – she kept quiet about it.

And 20 years ago, we also steered clear of talking openly about industrial policy. Instead, with our economy returning to full employment, we focussed on providing macroeconomic stability and reforms to increase competition, encourage enterprise, support science and improve skills.

But since the global financial crisis and following the pioneering work of Peter Mandelson as business secretary, a consensus has emerged that focusing on specific sectors is not only essential; it is inevitable.

Mike Wright's report on manufacturing and the supply chain made clear there is a clear role for government to give strategic direction, bring sectors together to foster long-term planning and tackle issues like the cost base and skills.

At a national level, we also need clear long-term direction. We need action, as George Cox's report said, on boardroom pay, and corporate governance.

We need more competition in banking and a British Investment Bank to support small and growing companies.

We badly need an independent infrastructure commission that can work to put aside the dither and squabbling that has dogged our approach to infrastructure for decades.

From Silicon Valley to the City of London, the world's best industries tend to be clustered. In the UK, our automotive sector is concentrated in the Midlands and north-east; the offshore wind sector brings jobs to many coastal regions; and aerospace is predominantly based in the north-west; and our creative industries are centred in major cities like London, Manchester, Bristol and Leeds. The government cannot create clusters – but it can do a lot to support those that already exist, especially at the local level.

But we also need a new long-term framework for science and innovation. Mike Wright and Andrew Adonis's reports both looked carefully at government support for innovation and science. They both come to similar conclusions, in particular that the 10-year framework for science funding, set up by David Sainsbury as science minister, provided the stability and long-termism that our research base and companies need.

I believe that a similar long-term funding framework for innovation policy, covering initiatives like the Technology Strategy Board and Catapult centres, will be equally important to delivering an inclusive prosperity.

CONCLUSION

This agenda for inclusive prosperity is pro-business, but not business as usual.

It demands we steer a midcourse between laissez-faire complacency on the one hand and protectionism and anti-Europeanism on the other.

It requires us to forge a long-term consensus to embrace open markets while actively working to secure the skills, long-term investment and market reforms we need to deliver rising prosperity for all.

And it recognises that if we are to maintain public support for an open market economy, we need to address public concerns, promote competition and long-term investment and make sure markets like energy and banking work better for consumers and businesses alike.

This is today's road to a new inclusive prosperity for the 21st century.

NOTE

1. This article is an edited version of a speech delivered by Ed Balls, as shadow chancellor, to the London Business School on 30 June 2014. It foreshadows the findings of the Inclusive Prosperity Commission, which Ed Balls chaired with former US Treasury Secretary Larry Summers and which reported in January 2015.

Part II

Economics: Innovation, Competitiveness and Smart Regulation

A DIGITAL PROGRESSIVE PROJECT

Karen Kornbluh

In the industrial economy of the late 19th and early 20th centuries, companies rationalised their processes to take advantage of capital investments with scale production. These new arrangements produced economic growth, but also major economic and social dislocation; many families moved to cities to take factory jobs and workers gave up farm life for a wage income. Companies amassed economic power, and inequality grew. Throughout Europe, a patchwork system of social insurance grew to soften the hard edges of the industrial economy for workers and their families by helping them share the risks associated with the inability of the breadwinner to earn the family income because of sickness, old age, a temporary layoff, or disability. Franklin Roosevelt borrowed the concept for the US's own version of social insurance. These systems, along with consumer protections and labour laws, helped bring about the great progressive triumph of middle class prosperity and dignity of the 20th century.

However, in the last few decades, as the digital revolution has disrupted the industrial economy, it has also disrupted middle class existence. Those who seek to restore economic security and combat growing inequality should look to the great innovation of the last century, social insurance, but update it to meet changed circumstances. They also should find ways to harness the new technologies to update the social sectors. Progressives should not attempt to put the digital genie back in the bottle, but instead look to reform progressive policies for the new digital age.

The OECD calls the internet "a great enabler", like electricity and the combustion engine before it. The internet connects and drives down the cost of transactions and collaboration. Suppliers link to designers, innovators to producers to consumers, dissidents and artists have outlets to reach a public that they could not previously have dreamed of reaching. The internet favours the edge over the centre and the lean over the large. In its initial stages in the 1990s it unleashed innovation, investment and productivity – driving up wages and employment.

However, the internet age, like the industrial age before it, has also resulted in great dislocation for families, workers, and communities. The internet accelerates globalisation by allowing companies to outsource many functions around the world and creates a 'winner-takes-all' economy that drives down wages and employment-related social insurance for workers in commoditised industries and jobs. It undermines the industrial age protections while transferring political and economic control to a highly educated few, who are able to leverage capital and other scarce resources.

Just as politicians are finally recognising the need to address these challenges, new technologies are changing business organisations again. Data science, artificial intelligence, and advanced automation will drive additional economic and social advances – and they will also introduce additional competition to labour, in the form of algorithms and robots.

As in the industrial age, the problem is not the technology or the business organisation, but a failure of policies. A new digital progressive project should reform industrial era policies to help broaden the benefits of the new age.

First, policy reform would remake the social insurance system for the new economy. Doing so offers the upside of unleashing the potential of an inclusive new digital economy and would restore economic security to working families. However, it runs the risk of ending the fragile ceasefire negotiated over the existence of these social insurance programmes, and for this reason it is not to be undertaken lightly. But as the UK Labour party warned in the 1990s about the British health system, these programmes must be reformed so that they remain relevant to the middle classes if they are to be saved.

The great social insurance programmes that underpin the economies of the major democracies were created in response to a transformative period analogous to the one we live in today. The US was late to social insurance policy, waiting until the exigencies of the Great Depression led Franklin Roosevelt to copy the programmes that had already grown up in Europe and were the subject of state-level experiments in the US. Bismarck's Germany led with a sickness law, workmen's compensation and compulsory old-age insurance – all created in the 1880s, and unemployment insurance finally in 1927. England's workmen's compensation law dated to 1880, though its sickness and unemployment insurance laws did not bear fruit until 1911, pushed along by Winston Churchill, and its old-age insurance system was not created until 1925. Denmark had been the first to institute a national old-age pension system followed by France, which in 1897 created an optional system that became compulsory in 1910; France had created voluntary unemployment insurance in 1905 and a sickness insurance law in 1930. These systems differed in how much of the contributions came from employers, employees and government, how premiums were computed, what benefit levels were, and what protections were included.

Social insurance has been one of the most successful government initiatives ever undertaken. The universality of these systems helped bond our societies together, while the progressive transfers kept inequality in check and kept the wolf from the door for families without a financial cushion when an assembly line closed, an injury occurred, or the breadwinner grew too old to work in the mill. As Roosevelt put it when he borrowed the model, these programmes helped guard against "the hazards and vicissitudes" of life in the new economy. They supplemented basic employment innovations like the creation of the minimum wage, limits on the working week, and the ban on child labour. The success and durability of capitalism in the 20th century cannot be separated from the success of social insurance.

In the new digital economy, social insurance programmes continue to provide families essential support. Yet because they were designed for a different economy, and in many instances a different family, they are in need of reform. Today, workers in developed countries face a volatile, 'winner-takes-all' economy. They compete with workers around the world for wages and benefits. They are increasingly employed in nonstandard positions – temporary, part-time, freelance, contingent, day labour, on-call, self-employed, or 'sharing'. They change jobs more frequently and are unemployed for longer periods than in the past. Employees today are less likely to be offered benefits through employers. Only those who have rare and needed assets to sell on the global market can earn large returns; those whose work can be done off-shore or by a machine have no such luck.

The family has changed as well. Today, most families with children are headed by either two working parents or a single parent who works. Parents in these new 'juggler families' are working more and more hours, but wages have stagnated, and so they are running harder just to stay in place. For these families, juggling to make ends meet, time off to care for a sick relative can result in devastating income interruptions and even job loss. As a result, juggler parents often wind up paying a hefty penalty just to be good parents. They lose jobs as a result of a child's illness; they take part-time, contingent, or other nonstandard jobs; and they sacrifice wages, benefits, and job security if they cannot do shift work.

The challenges differ in the US and Europe. The US finally has universal health insurance, filling its greatest social insurance gap, but workers still lack family and medical leave insurance (the ability to take leave with pay for a new child, an illness, or to care for an ill relative) as well as subsidised childcare – areas in which much of Europe's social insurance system has kept up with the changing family. These are especially important since American families often have little control over or even advanced knowledge of their work schedule and one third of children live in families with only a single parent. In addition, where American social insurance takes the form of a tax-subsidised employer benefit – as in pensions – major holes have opened. In Europe, far more generous policies for childcare, family leave, and poverty prevention prevail. However, ageing populations, slow growth, youth unemployment, and austerity politics put tremendous financial pressure on European social programmes and subject them to criticism for supporting existing workers – with early retirement or long periods of unemployment insurance – at the expense of new ones, including youth and immigrants.

The answer to these challenges is not that social insurance should be privatised. Rather, it must be reformed to share the new risks families bear and lessen the inequalities created by the new 'winner-takes-all' economy. This should be the central goal for progressives in the 21st century.

What is needed are new universal insurance schemes that fill the new gaps in the system that provide workers no margin for error. These programmes would be tied not to work for a paternalistic employer (as is often the case in the US programmes) or only to citizenship (as is the case with many programmes in Europe), but to activities that contribute to society, such as job training and childrearing.

A new family insurance system is needed in the US.[1] It would enable families to draw down benefits to replace earning lost as a result of taking leave up to a capped amount, just as they do in retirement. The benefits could replace partial earnings if a worker goes part-time instead of taking full-time leave – including if he or she decides to take part of his or her child leave as reduced leave. Family insurance would include an add-on account. New parent accounts would cover the health, childcare, and education-related expenses of raising a child.

A new training insurance system is needed to provide training and income support for mid-career workers who lose a job, and young people. Benefits would subsidise on-the-job internships and worker training programmes. These would need to be added on to existing unemployment insurance schemes to guarantee a sufficiently broad pool to cover new workers coming into the system. To be eligible, programme providers would be required to submit to rigorous assessments of outcomes they produce.

Other new insurance policies could plug other gaps in the industrial era social insurance systems in various countries, eg for pensions or disability disrupted by 'sharing economy' work.

Funds for these inequality-fighting insurance policies would be assessed on a progressive basis (unlike with US social security, where one's first dollar earned is subject to tax). Regressive or outdated benefits, such as the flexible spending tax benefit in the US, available only to those with taxable income and a good employer, might be sacrificed over time.

Citizens are ahead of politicians in realising the system has failed to keep up. If they do not hear solutions from progressives they will be more likely to respond to arguments for dismantling the whole enterprise and lowering taxes. This may be especially true of both of those who have little hope of being cut into the system and those who feel they do not need it. However, the effort of filling the gaps in social insurance must be undertaken with great transparency so as not to appear to cheat current workers and retirees of the benefits they have been promised – and relied on – through their working lives.

A successful digital progressive project will also need reform at its centre, and should follow the lead of former New York City mayor Michael Bloomberg, who demonstrated his seriousness by cutting programmes that failed effectiveness tests, and French prime minister Manuel Valls, who eliminated an array of outdated business restrictions. Without a plan to reform existing programmes, the call for new social protections sounds to many anxious voters like a call for government to play a larger role in the economy and undermine growth. The progressive paradox holds: voters' hostility to government programmes often increases in hard times because government seems less effective at addressing their needs and a smaller tax bill seems preferable. A recent US study supports this thesis – showing, for example, declining US voter support for Obamacare even as inequality rises.

Therefore, a second group of necessary policy reforms would harness the technologies of the future to improve the delivery of social services. Digital technology has improved service delivery in most industries with the exception of the social sectors such as education, health care, energy and the operation of government itself. Teacher and student, nurse and patient, public servant and citizen are left behind in an industrial-age top-down, one-size-fits-all environment without the personalised, connected, information-rich tools that have unleashed so much creativity for consumers.

In education and training, new technologies offer the opportunity for tailored, wrap-around learning at home and at school, as well as the ability to train for and find new jobs in the digital economy. National programmes can ensure high-speed broadband reaches all classrooms and homes with children and they can also train teachers in the use of the new technology tools and spread best practices for the use of technology. In health care, telemedicine can be deployed to enable video consultation and remote patient monitoring while electronic health records can improve quality and reduce costs. Technology can improve energy distribution, as in Estonia where advanced smart meters allow utilities to track customer consumption on an hourly basis. Then, by logging into a friendly, web-based interface, customers can in turn see their detailed metering results and adjust their usage accordingly.

In the operation of government itself, technology can enhance transparency, accountability, responsiveness, and effectiveness. A new 'mobile-first' government with a 'customer-centric' approach is needed. Citizens should be as empowered in their dealings with the government, just as they are as customers – casting a ballot from the comfort of their own living room, filing income tax returns in just five minutes, signing a legally-binding contract over the Internet from anywhere in the world via a mobile phone, registering new businesses in as little as 20 minutes. For example, in Kansas City, Missouri, new business owners use an online tool to help navigate complex regulations and approval processes in place of the old system in which business owners were expected to identify which permits they would need and work with multiple departments.

Programmes should be monitored for effectiveness; those that do not work should be ended or reformed, and those that do should be celebrated and funded to scale. Digital technology is already unleashing new growth and opportunity for some, but will strengthen our societies only if we learn how to reform our industrial age policies so that these technologies fuel a new wave of prosperity and dignity.

NOTE

1. I first proposed Family Insurance in my 2006 article 'Families Valued: Creating a 21st century social insurance system for today's "juggler families"' in the journal *Democracy*.

THE DIGITAL ECONOMY – A PLATFORM FOR CENTRE-LEFT REVIVAL?

Paul Hofheinz

Who are 'progressives'? What are the values that unite us and make us who and what we are?

One of the first characteristics is an approach to 'the modern', a belief that the future is a challenge to be embraced and not a curse to be avoided. This, more than anything, defines the now 230-year-old movement which began when Immanuel Kant argued that the shift from barbarism to civilization was a historic trend which society would be well advised to embrace, and could sensibly serve as a rallying point around which future political movements could be formed.[1] The struggle for such an embrace of change continues to this day. As you read these words, centre-left parties around the world are debating their roots and core values. What agenda can unite society around a common vision of progress? How can we articulate this vision in ways that are electorally convincing and economically effective? And most importantly, what are the policies we should promote, the ones that will give us the growth, jobs and social inclusion we are committed to deliver and upon which we will be judged?

These are not easy questions, and in some ways they are what make our progressive debates so fascinating. Certainly, they inspire some of the modern world's greatest minds to weigh in, taking on political themes that might have seemed too mundane had these central intellectual challenges not been so prominent in them.[2] Put simply, we progressives face a tall order. Conceived on the value-laden left, we have a politics that seeks to harness the power of the state to deliver social wellbeing but never lets the state become an impediment to progress itself; which exists beyond the interest-group capture that has become the rock upon which so many parties have perished (left and right); that develops and implements a strategy uniting the many who work for a better tomorrow; that puts the interests of none above the welfare of the many; that speaks truth to power; and that wins elections and governs well when we do win them. Fundamentally, we are committed to doing the right thing. So what is the 'right thing'? What can we do that will give us the growth, jobs and greater equality we seek?

Society is going through a wrenching transition at present. It is not so much that technology has propelled us prematurely into a future of disruption and not-so-creative destruction, but rather that we can scarcely understand the present in which we live. Despite the steady drip of negative headlines, and some harrowing electoral reversals in key places, it is decidedly not a negative present. Indeed, the seeds and tools of tomorrow's success are all around us, should we be bold enough to plant and seize them today. Consider this: whatever doom the naysayers are forecasting, digital technology has already created more opportunity for more people than any technological change since the arrival of the printing press some 500 years ago.[3] It is a general purpose technology, whose role and presence permeates the economy, which brings an end to centuries-old industries in some places, but gives rise to dramatically improved and hugely popular goods and services in others.[4] It is a great social leveller – putting resources formerly available to the few in the hands of the many.[5] Most notably, it may well be the sole concession to a better life that this generation has successfully bequeathed to the next.[6]

Children love technology. We might not be able to give them jobs when they leave school or university, but we have given them a future. To be blunt, that future is in the digital world, which they take (rightly) to be their birthright. Children are not like their parents; they no longer watch much television, they find the 'copyright wars' we adults engage in amusingly quaint. Even if we have not really been able to pass on the promise of social advancement that our generation took for granted, at least we have been able to give them this: an exciting new platform they will use to rewrite the rules of democratic engagement.[7]

This is why the digital agenda can and must become a central plank of any modern, progressive agenda. Digital technology, and the economic and social revolution it brings in its wake, is the future. It creates more jobs than it destroys, and it allows for better, more reasoned policymaking at all levels, from the individual to the state.[8] Any effort to put our society and our policies on the wrong side of digital advancement – and there are powerful interests on the left and right pushing us hard to go there – will only condemn the proponents to a fate not unlike the Spanish Inquisition – powerful enough to win the discussion of the day, but sufficiently out of touch to lose the long-term argument forever.

So what, then, does a progressive digital agenda look like? I would argue that there are two separate but equally important components: one rhetorical, the other programmatic.

First and foremost, concerning the rhetorical, the centre left must tread more carefully on the digital agenda. We must redouble our efforts not to let the newness and challenge of successfully managing the social disruption brought by the new business models and technology – and, frankly, the not always progressive views of some parts of our base – put us in an electorally losing corner here. We should – to be direct about it – stop scaring everyone about digital technology. Certainly, there is disruption involved; but since when were progressives people who thought a better world tomorrow should be stopped because of political exigency today? We must be careful how we set and defend our own red lines. This is particularly true in the key and vital area of data – called by some the 'oil' or the 'currency' of the new economy. Regardless of the metaphor, it is the essential input that the digital economy needs to operate – the way that modern businesses communicate, the raw material for developing and forming better insights about society that are the essence of a progressive, evidence-based agenda.[9] The fact is, we need a progressive policy on data – one which enables the collection, retention, analysis and sharing of data, and one which helps us integrate in international markets, where we are destined to thrive if only we would embrace the challenge and let ourselves fully compete. We must move forward with a political stance that says, yes, privacy will be protected; but we reject a political stance in which we declare the glue that holds the internet together to be a toxic substance, most safely kept secure within not-even-faintly protectionist national borders.

Second of all, the programmatic: digital technology does mean disruption, and who is better positioned to manage disruption in a convincing and socially fair way than progressives? We need the jobs that come with digital technology, to be frank about the matter. The political process today is overshadowed by a persistently sluggish recovery that no one can or should be pleased with. The winner will be the party that cobbles together an electoral programme that convincingly offers new jobs and sustainable economic growth. In an advanced economy, this means first and foremost embracing the outer edge of top-level economic development, what the Germans have called *Industrie 4.0* – or the fourth industrial revolution. As well as this though, we should establish and embrace a culture of entrepreneurship, of startups, of new business services and models, a culture of experimentation and innovation, and a society where every individual is encouraged to succeed and given the tools to do so. We should embrace the merger of industry and services using our fundamental strengths in both areas to make Europe a place where the businesses of tomorrow thrive, are diffused, and generate enough sustainable employment to put an end to the near permanent angst that today's generation feels. We need a culture of readily available and ongoing education, a society where hard and soft skills unite with the distributive power of the internet to foment and abet a life unlike any other that has ever been lived. Most notably, we should approach voters with the idea that, yes, we understand this is difficult. But our party has a comprehensive programme, a social compact, which we will implement to make sure that we are capable of building the jobs and driving the growth right here at home, where we will thrive in the digital era.[10]

To conclude, this is not an entirely new idea. In fact, it is what propelled Harold Wilson to electoral victory in 1964. With a campaign based on embracing the 'white heat of technology', he felled two beasts with one rhetorical sword: he positioned Labour as the party of the modern, and he cast the hapless Tories of the time as the party of yesterday, with no ideas, and an agenda that smelled more of mothballs than silicon chips.

The magic is there again for the reaching, but to get there we must move quickly and decisively – and sincerely. For an internet-abetted population – one where Twitter carries more weight than the chattering classes of London, Paris, Washington or Berlin – loathes nothing more than craven grabs for power and the perceived insincerity of politicians uttering shibboleths in which they hardly believe. This puts an onus on doing our homework. It is vital that we understand the digital agenda, that we see how it can and will help our society to advance and that we embrace it publicly with the enthusiasm and confidence of a millennial.[11]

Such an approach though requires tolerance, vision and courage – political virtues that are not in great supply today. It helps that we have a long and powerful tradition of being the first to see the future, and the first to embrace that future and give it political expression in the contemporary context. But we are not doing that today. We remain – on this and in many other areas – caught up in the electoral logic of the industrial age. It is a challenge that has defined progressives throughout the ages, and not coincidentally determined our political success as well.

NOTES

1. Kant, I. (1795) *Perpetual Peace: A Philosophical Sketch.*
2. Giddens, A. (1998) *The Third Way: The Renewal of Social Democracy*, Cambridge: Polity Press.

3. Shirky, C. (2008) *Here Comes Everybody: The Power of Organising Without Organisations*, London: Penguin.

4. Mettler, A. & Williams, A. D. (2011) 'The Rise of the Micro-Multinational: How Freelancers and Technology-Savvy Startups are Driving Growth Jobs and Innovation', *Lisbon Council Policy Brief*, 5(3); See also: Mettler, A. & Williams, A. D. (2012) 'Wired for Growth and Innovation: How Digital Technologies are Reshaping Small- and Medium-Sized Businesses', *Interactive Policy Brief*, Brussels: The Lisbon Council.

5. Aghion, P., Akcigit, U., Bergeaud, A., Blundell, R. & Hemous, D. (2015) 'Innovation, Income Inequality and Social Mobility', *Vox EU*, 28 July 2015.

6. Mandel, M. & Carew, D. (2015) 'Tech Opportunity for Minorities and Women: A Good News, Bad News Story', *Policy Memo*, Washington DC: Progressive Policy Institute.

7. Filippov, S. (2015) 'Government of the Future: How Digital Technology Will Change the Way We Live, Work and Government', *European Digital Forum Digital Insight*, Brussels & London: The Lisbon Council & Nesta.

8. A study of census results in England and Wales since 1871 finds that technology has been a job creator rather than making working humans obsolete. See: Stewart, I. De, D. & Cole, A. (2015) *Technology and People: The Great Job-Creating Machine*, London: Deloitte.

9. Hofheinz, P. & Mandel, M. (2015) 'Uncovering the Hidden Value of Digital Trade: Towards a 21st Century Agenda of Transatlantic Prosperity', *Interactive Policy Brief, 19/2015*, Brussels & Washington DC: The Lisbon Council & Progressive Policy Institute.

10. In a previous essay, I argued that a progressive innovation agenda should be based on four key principals: (1) Build, (2) Educate, (3) Open and (4) Learn. See: Hofheinz, P. (2015) 'An Innovation Agenda for Europe' in: Atkinson, R. D., McTernan, M. & Reed, A. [Eds.] *Sharing in the Success of the Digital Economy: A Progressive Approach to Radical Innovation*, Washington DC & London: Information Technology and Innovation Foundation & Policy Network.

11. For an interesting account of the role of social media in Barack Obama's first presidential campaign, see: Harfoush, R. (2009) *Yes We Did*, Washington DC: New Riders; Gertner, J. (2015) 'Inside Obama's Stealth Startup', *Fast Company*.

WOMEN'S LABOUR MARKET PARTICIPATION – CONTINUING CHALLENGES IN SWEDEN

Moira Nelson and Dalia Mukhtar-Landgren

Two common objectives of governments today – high employment and fertility – are difficult to achieve at the same time if parents feel like they cannot balance work with family life. In efforts to reduce these trade-offs many governments have expanded parental leave schemes and daycare. Sweden is often pointed to as an example of best practice and high levels of employment coupled with relatively high fertility rates appear to confirm that the ability of these policies to resolve tensions between work and family and enable women to gain an equal foothold in the labour market in many respects. Yet closer inspection of the Swedish case demonstrates how challenges persist in terms of women's labour market participation and therein their economic wellbeing. The persistence of involuntary part-time work, especially, hinders their earnings capacity which then weakens their access to social insurance rights and increases their risk of poverty. The space that follows reviews these ongoing challenges in order to inform the work of governments aiming to improve women's economic wellbeing.

Before turning to the challenges that persist in Sweden, it is worth clarifying the particular policy reforms that facilitate work-life reconciliation.[1] An obligatory two-week maternity leave before and after the birth exists. Each family is eligible to 480 days' paid leave (and unlimited unpaid leave for the first 18 months). For 390 days, the compensation is based on the person's income and the other 90 days the compensation is reduced to 180 SEK per day (the so-called 'days at the minimum level'). A *jämställdhetsbonus* (gender equality bonus), enacted in 2008 and discontinued as of 2017, provides extra money to parents with children born after 1 July 2008 who split the 390 leave days evenly. There has been some scepticism as to whether this bonus encourages equality. An evaluation study conducted by the Swedish Social Insurance Agency[2] indicated that the bonus has not prompted parents to change their behaviour: a comparison between a group born two weeks before and two weeks after 1 July 2008 shows that fathers in both groups have on average taken out about 44 days of parental leave, while the mothers took out 249–250 days. The Social Insurance Agency lists a number of possible explanations for this: (i) it can take time for a reform to grow on the public, (ii) rules and requirements might have been too complex, (iii) parents receive the bonus retroactively, and (iv) parents base their decision on factors other than purely economic one, such as prevailing gender norms, values and traditions but also power relations and personal experiences.[3] According to Statistics Sweden, fathers' share of parental leave amounted to 25 per cent in 2014, up from 12 per cent in 2000, but this was arguably not the result of the bonus.[4] Germany provides an interesting base of comparison because Swedish style parental leave came into effect in 2007. In Germany, fathers' share stood at 21.1 per cent for completed benefit periods of those with children born from 2013 onwards, according to the German Federal Statistical Office. To encourage flexibility of use, paid leave is counted in days, may be used until the child is 12 years old, and taken full-time, half-time, quarter-time or one-eighth time.[5] Parents with children of up to eight years old also have the right to reduce working time by 25 per cent. As a result parents can choose to 'save' a number of their days in order to reduce working hours and still protect their eligibility in relation to social insurance such as unemployment and sickness benefits. In this regard a parent can choose to work 80 per cent and be on parental leave on 20 per cent – and still be covered 100 per cent by his/her social insurance. When the 480 days are finished the parent can continue to work part time – but his/her eligibility to social insurance will be impaired. Municipalities are required to provide full-time preschool to children aged one to six for parents who hold employment. Municipalities also provide other potentially relevant social services such as care for elderly and disabled family members. A municipality-based childcare allowance was also re-established in 2008 and offered up to €320 per month to parents who did not use public daycare.[6] This allowance was optional for municipalities, and it was later on abolished in February 2016. Whereas this last policy receives criticism for weakening incentives for mothers to enter the labour market, the remaining policies are all broadly seen as supporting the labour market ambitions of mothers and therein their economic independence and social integration.

The Swedish family policy mix certainly functions to improve women's ability to participate in the labour market. But while still exceptional in international comparison Sweden falls short of providing women with an equal foothold in the labour market. Occupational segregation is high, with women much more likely to work in the public sector. About 70 per cent of the public sector workforce is female in Sweden and the public sector absorbs about half of the female workforce. The barriers to private sector work follows from the belief that many of these jobs are better suited to men. Even in Sweden there continues to be this type of gender essentialism or the treatment of women's work as fundamentally different from men's work. This is also indicated by segregation between the sexes in the education system: 76 per cent of the women in upper secondary school (and 23 per cent of men) were enrolled in women-dominated programmes. This is only a small improvement since 1986 were the corresponding number were 80 per cent of the women and 23 per cent of the men.[7] There is an ongoing debate over whether discrimination against women in Sweden is stronger in the public versus the private sector, although there is recent evidence of trends towards desegmentation.[8]

Overall, public sector employment is often seen as rather attractive to women, although there are also downsides. In particular, involuntary part-time work is a large problem. The greater availability of part-time work in the public sector as well as the service sector enables many women to combine work and care. Nevertheless, many other women would prefer full-time work but can only find part-time work. In 2013 30 per cent of all women worked part time in Sweden.[9] The OECD statistical database reveals that 32.6 per cent of part-time workers are involuntary part-timers, which is also supported by in the statistical review *Women and Men in Sweden* where the primary reason for part-time employment is "cannot find suitable full-time work".[10] Even though voluntary part time is also common amongst Swedish women with small children (where eg 48 per cent of women with two small children work part time), the number of women who cannot find a full-time job has increased since 2005 and "[t]he most common type for women in both 1987 and 2013 was a temporary replacement position".[11]

Beyond the promise and peril of public sector work, a high gender pay gap also remains in Sweden and does not differ substantially from the European average. In 2011 women earned about 15.8 per cent less than men according to Eurostat. Part but not all of this gap can be explained by the type and amount of work that women do as compared to men. Beyond identifying some jobs or tasks as inherently female or male, there is also an ongoing tendency to undervalue women's work and such bias may be exercised by various people such as employers or even women themselves.

The inability to find full-time work has a number of disadvantages. Part-time work often involves lower pay than full-time work such that the high incidence of part-time work among women has a clear influence on women's earnings and risk of poverty. These differences between men and women often hold implications for the level of social insurance benefits for which workers are eligible. This is often noted in relation to pensions where women on average receive approximately 66 per cent of what men receive,[12] and where we today have a growing percentage of female pensioners who are under or just above the EU poverty threshold (60 per cent of national median equivalised disposable income). Even though women in Sweden often have a long working life behind them, the economic reality for male and female pensioners differ radically in Sweden today, as about 70 per cent of those with incomes below the EU poverty line are women.[13] In reviews from trade unions this is often explained by the high incidence of part-time work, lower salaries (due to sector and the gender pay gap), as well as a longer break from work in relation to having children.

Further, the relationship between the family, labour market and welfare state is shifting with cutbacks in the welfare state. Extensive social services such as daycare, care of the elderly and disabled have been central to women's ability to participate in the labour market often described in terms of the Nordic 'women-friendly' welfare state. Today a growing literature is describing the transition from the defamilarised Nordic welfare state to a process of "refamilisation" as the responsibilites for childen, elderly and sick are being reversed back to the family primarily women as a result of cutbacks in the welfare state.[14] These changes are related both to quality and (to a lesser extent) accessibility. Important to note in this regard is that accessibility is not the only factor affecting women's choice, but the quality of the services provided is also central and affects women's choices in terms of part- and full-time work. This also opens up the question of inequalities between different women, where we know that accessibility to high-quality alternatives – as well as the possibility to choose private alternatives such as nanny's or au pairs – vary in relation to class and/or ethnic background. Cutbacks in the welfare state therefore affect women both as employees and as care-givers.

Improving women's economic wellbeing therefore calls for much more change than family policies that enable work-life reconciliation. As the Swedish case demonstrates, ongoing barriers to private sector jobs need to be removed, the availability of full-time positions in the public sector and service sector improved and high quality social services must be made available.

NOTES

1. Duvander, A. Z., Haas, L. & C. P. Hwaang (2015) 'Sweden country note', in: P. Moss (ed.) *International Review of Leave Policies and Research*, http://www.leavenetwork.org/lp_and_r_reports/.

2. The Swedish Social Insurance Agency (2010) 'The gender equality bonus – An impact evaluation' (Jämställdhetsbonusen: en effektutvärdering), *Social Insurance Report 2010:* 5. https://www.forsakringskassan.se/wps/wcm/connect/249a8f02-6e59-4337-aa1b-0c109671ea22/socialforsakringsrapport_2010_5.pdf?MOD=AJPERES.

3. Ibid.

4. Cromas, M. (2015) 'The gender equality bonus will be abolished in 2017' (Jämställdhetsbonus slopas 2017), *Dagens Nyhete*, http://www.dn.se/ekonomi/jamstalldhetsbonus-slopas-2017/ 15/09/2016.

5. Gunnarsson, L., Korpi, B. M., & Nordenstam, U. (2000) *Early Childhood Education and Care Policy in Sweden*. Stockholm: Ministry of Education and Science Stockholm.

6. Duvander, A. Z., Haas, L. & C. P. Hwaang (2015) 'Sweden country note', http://www.leavenetwork.org/lp_and_r_reports/.

7. SCB (2014) 'Women and men in Sweden: Facts and figures 2014', *Statistics Sweden*. http://www.scb.se/Statistik/_Publikationer/LE0201_2013B14_BR_X10BR1401ENG.pdf: 5.

8. Ellingsæter, A. L. (2013) 'Scandinavian welfare states and gender (de) segregation: Recent trends and processes', *Economic and Industrial Democracy* 34(3): 501–18.

9. SCB (2014) 'Women and men in Sweden: Facts and figures 2014 Statistics Sweden'. Available at: http://www.scb.se/Statistik/_Publikationer/LE0201_2013B14_BR_X10BR1401ENG.pdf: 57.

10. Ibid.: 59; Björnberg, U. & Dahlgren, L. (2003) 'Labour Supply–the case of Sweden'. Social Policy Research Unit, University of York. *Welfare Policies and Employment in the Context of Family Change*.

11. SCB (2014) 'Women and men in Sweden: Facts and figures 2014 Statistics Sweden'. Available at: http://www.scb.se/Statistik/_Publikationer/LE0201_2013B14_BR_X10BR1401ENG.pdf: 63.

12. SCB (2014) 'Women and men in Sweden: Facts and figures 2014 Statistics Sweden'. Available at: http://www.scb.se/Statistik/_Publikationer/LE0201_2013B14_BR_X10BR1401ENG.pdf.

13. PRO (2015) Ålderdom utan fattigdom: om äldrefattigdom och kvinnors låga pensioner [Ageing without poverty: on older women's poverty and low pensions], *Swedish National Pensioners' Organisation*: 16.

14. Borchorst, A. & Siims, B. (2008) 'Women-friendly policies and state feminism', *Feminist Theory* 9(2): 207–24.

GENERAL REFERENCE

Åsa, L. (2011) *Family Policy Paradoxes. Gender Equality and Labour Market Regulation in Sweden, 1930–2010.* Great Britain: Policy Press.

FUELLING FUTURE GROWTH IN EUROPE

Carlotta de Franceschi

It is not by augmenting the capital of the country, but by render-
ing a greater part of that capital active and productive than would
otherwise be so, that the most judicious operations of banking
can increase the industry of the country.

– Adam Smith

It has been seven years since the Lehman collapse, the event which
dragged the world into the worst economic and financial crisis since
the Great Depression. Despite small signs of recovery, Europe is
akin to a team of clumsy football players glimpsing at its nimble
global rivals with a mix of worry, envy and puzzlement.

European governments have been talking about spurring growth
for quite a while, but have not yet been able to come up with a
shared and organic reform agenda for one of the key determinants
for growth: finance.

If we think about the broader financial system as a power grid
that fuels companies and new ideas, progressives should focus on
making the power stations (the banking system, capital markets
and alternative finance) more effective as well as improving those
frameworks (bankruptcy and tax) that, like switches, enable the grid
to become a catalyst for new jobs creation.

As for the banking system, progressives should aim to correct some of the overreach of the recent regulation and of the way Basel III was implemented in Europe, as well as the pursuit of a fast development of securitisation with the joint effort to strengthen domestic public guarantee programmes. This will enable banks to effectively serve the real economy as well as fully transfer the benefits of European Central Bank (ECB) policy onto SMEs.

Progressives should also take the canvas provided by the capital markets union as an opportunity to advocate for a set of policies that makes our capital markets as well as our alternative finance channels more developed and integrated. This will provide our economies with a powerful breath of new oxygen and make our companies more competitive in the global arena.

Following domestic bank rescues in 2008, and faced with angry tax payers, policymakers reacted fast and regulated the banking system by implementing the Basel III framework sooner and more strictly than in the US. As a result, European banks started a massive deleveraging that hurt SMEs as well as families. Even if the original intention was good, the effect of this decision on employment and domestic deficits was not.

The results of the new banking policy were particularly harsh on the European real economy for two reasons: first of all, when compared to US companies that can count on well-developed and deep capital markets, European ones get their financing mostly through the banking sector; second of all, SMEs, which make up about 60 per cent of European GDP and account for about 70 per cent of European employment, struggle to finance through capital markets as opposed to banks. So, mostly by design, while the US in the recovery could leverage two lungs (a developed capital market and a banking sector that could postpone deleveraging – note also that Basel III does not apply to US regional banks), Europe could only rely on a weakened one (a troubled banking sector in deleveraging). In other words, the banking policy that aimed at protecting taxpayers ended up smothering those real economies that, to the same tax payers, provide directly for employment and indirectly for welfare packages.

As for the banking policy, fixing it should be a priority; it takes time for policymakers to develop capital markets and alternative finance channels, and for companies to change funding patterns. Progressives should therefore revise the overreaching points of the regulation and advocate for a shift in perspective from stability to sustainability. At the same time, progressives should put securitisation at the centre of their agenda as a tool to improve the flow of credit and reduce its costs to the real economy and in particular to SMEs. The problem with SMEs is that they are smaller, less transparent, less liquid of an investment and often less creditworthy than larger companies, making them less suited for non-bank financing. If we think of the ECB as a well providing water to European economies and of SMEs as remote villages, securitisation could actually be the powerful network of channels that carry the ECB's water to the villages. In order to make the network channel really pervasive and watertight, the European commission and domestic governments should work together to enhance the public sector guarantee programmes across Europe. While doing so, progressives should ask for a wider availability of European structural funds and more fiscal flexibility to support these programmes. By providing an easier access to the ECB liquidity, public sector guarantee programmes will make our economies immune to future sovereign and capital markets crisis.

As for capital markets and alternative finance, it is a widespread view that if Europe wants to foster growth, it can no longer largely rely on banks to provide for financing and has to further develop and integrate these channels. Strengthening capital markets and alternative finance will also make our corporate sector less dependent on banks and our banking sector more resilient to crisis.

On 30 September 2015, the European commission launched an action plan to execute this vision. As we all know, the devil of this policy will be in the details and while progressives tackle these details, they should not miss the vision for the long term. In particular, progressives should not fear to be ambitious: does the urgency of the matter require a radical approach or, like the one the European commission action plan seems to suggest, an incremental approach?

Especially when facing considerations like supervision (national versus single), which is a key ingredient of an effective and rapid market integration, policy answers are not trivial. As Nicolas Véron points out, the roll out of a single market initiative in unregulated products happens by the elimination of cross-border barriers, while in regulated services, like the financial sector, the enforcement functions (licensing, authorisation and supervision) involve considerable judgment and discretion. Therefore, a key policy decision to achieve rapidly cross-border integration would be to pool these functions at European level and leave a role to the national authorities of local and delegated operations. A less radical step would be to pool these functions at a European level, at least for the alternative finance channels (funds direct lending to SMEs and for peer-to-peer platforms), where the regulation is fairly new and far from being harmonised in its roll-out across Europe.

Furthermore, the reform agenda of progressives cannot overlook the role of pension funds and insurance companies. As a matter of fact, if the ECB is like a well that brings finance to companies through banks, then pension funds and insurers are like wells serving the same function through public as well as private capital markets and infrastructure investments. In particular, progressives cannot deny the priority of reframing the new insurance regulation (Solvency II). The new regime, largely inspired by the prudential one for banks, fails to take into account the long-term nature of insurance investments. By hampering the investment in equities and alternative investment funds, Solvency II eliminates from both public and private capital markets a whole segment of key players that are vital to fuel our economies.

As mentioned earlier, if we think of the financial system, capital markets and alternative finance as power stations in the grid that fuels corporate activity, both bankruptcy and tax regimes are the switches that enable the grid to actually create jobs.

In particular, bankruptcy frameworks affect the ability of a country to foster entrepreneurship, attract investors, sustain employment and provide a positive environment for companies to compete internationally (bankruptcy frameworks affect the overall cost of borrowing, the allocation of capital in the economy and the ability of companies to react and overcome crisis). The European commission is working to harmonise the different frameworks across the EU. From this perspective, progressives should share a common vision of broad pillars to spur entrepreneurship, to create a positive environment for innovative firms and to make companies in general more resilient to crisis. Progressives should therefore pursue a common reform agenda that would make it easier and less penalising for entrepreneurs who fail to try again and start new companies, that support viable companies to restructure their debt and that makes it cheaper and quicker for non-viable companies to finalise a bankruptcy process.

As for the tax regimes, if the objective is to encourage the investment in innovative firms, progressives should propose a reform agenda that is organic and encompasses entrepreneurs, employees, retail investors, institutional investors and corporates. In particular, progressive should advocate for a favourable tax treatment of equity compensation, such as stock options. Such a policy will provide high-growth companies with a valuable currency to attract and retain skilled talent. Progressives should also provide a favourable tax treatment for dividend and capital gains of founders and investors in new innovative companies and seek tax discrimination between long- and short-term investments (as it is in the US). Second, drawing on the European's best practices, progressives should promote the development of investment products that are suitable to retail investors and liquid for them to invest in innovative SMEs. It is worthwhile supporting these products with tax incentives to allow for the development of markets in the venture capital and dedicated public equity space. Finally, in a context of open innovation, progressives should make the acquisition or investment innovative companies by medium and larger ones tax deductible. This will make it cheaper for our corporates to acquire new technologies and will allow Europe to retain its leading innovative companies.

Some people may wonder whether the progressives' reform agenda should include some sort of social safety nets for entrepreneurs who bear the risk of starting up a new company. I do not believe social safety nets are a priority for entrepreneurs. What entrepreneurs ask for is the removal of the social stigma associated with failure paired with some sort of comfort that if they fail they will actually be able to start something back again within reasonable time, a positive environment to work and a good upside potential when their company turns into a success. Moving resources away from a favourable treatment of capital gains and dividends could actually drive entrepreneurship into the wrong people and force the ones we really want to migrate to the US or other more competitive landscapes.

Matteo Renzi's experience proves that sometimes to make a big step forward, countries should completely change direction. Why not be more ambitious then, especially in a field that would allow Europe to unlock its best human capital potential and fuel growth? Why not be brave, and pursue a radical rather than an incremental set of reforms? Progressives should create the conditions for its entrepreneurial class to flourish and create employment, to be rewarded rather than punished when trying something new and to have a pervasive and easy access to finance for the implementation of new ideas. This effort requires a great vision and a gear shift toward the development and integration of finance in Europe. A powerful policy agenda to fuel growth in our economies encompasses banks, insurance companies, pension funds, retail investors, financial products, capital markets infrastructure and supervision, bankruptcy and tax regimes across the EU. In the US people say: 'If you want to go fast, run alone, but if you want to go far, run together'. Maybe it is time for Europe to wear a common shirt and tackle this match as a real team, not clumsy this time, but on the same level playing field as its global rivals.

CREATIVE DESTRUCTION AND THE CHANGING GEOGRAPHY OF EUROPEAN JOBS

Thor Berger

European labour markets have been fundamentally transformed as digital technology has destroyed a wide range of routine jobs, while creating new employment opportunities for highly skilled workers. Recent technological breakthroughs may further exacerbate already rising regional inequalities, with some places pulling ahead and others left behind. A key challenge for policymakers is to devise policies that address the problems of regions that are struggling to adapt to the digital revolution. Policies should focus on improving digital literacy, while also fostering creative and high-level technical skills, enabling lagging areas to transform new technologies into new jobs, which would boost regional competitiveness in the digital age.

GROWING DIGITAL DIVIDES?

Major technological revolutions have always been associated with some places pulling ahead while others are left behind. Over past decades, metropolitan regions such as Berlin, London, and Stockholm have surged ahead by transforming the technologies of the digital revolution into new industries and jobs. At the same time, former manufacturing cities – once the prospering places of the industrial age – have struggled to reinvent themselves as a wide range of routine work has become automated.

Urban areas – with their dense economic activity – are becoming hubs of development because they connect the entrepreneurs, innovators and investors that are required to create jobs in the 21st century. Against the backdrop of increased communication and transportation affordability, the continued importance of physical proximity offered in these cities may seem counterintuitive. However, although mobile devices, social networks, and high-speed wireless broadband makes communication over vast distances possible at nearly zero cost, face-to-face interactions are still the key engine of innovation and growth.

In the long run, regions grow by creating entirely new types of jobs and industries. Whether it is the shift from agricultural work to the assembly line, or the more recent transition from manufacturing towards knowledge-intensive services, the creation of new work has been central to maintain growth. Indeed, the digital revolution has given birth to a wide range of new jobs for app developers, software designers, and search engine optimisers. Places that have managed to create these kinds of jobs have been growing faster as a result. New hi-tech industries, however, tend to be highly concentrated. In the UK, for example, new types of work are typically created in London and spread only slowly to less tech avant-garde places. An important challenge for policymakers is therefore to stimulate the creation of new jobs in areas that have seen the slowest change.

To transition into the jobs of the 21st century, workers need to acquire skills that justify their employment in the digital age. According to estimates from the European commission, there may be as many as 1 million vacancies in IT jobs already next year, reflecting a shortfall of workers with high-level technical skills. Regions that manage to either attract workers with such skillsets or provide opportunities for their inhabitants to acquire them are well positioned to see acceleration in growth. Stimulating hi-tech employment growth is important because it constitutes the most dynamic part of the European economy, but also because each additional job in the hi-tech sector creates as many as four additional jobs in the local economy.

REGIONAL POLICY: PEOPLE OR PLACES?

Policymakers have two options to address regional disparities: invest in people or places. Above all, policies should focus on upgrading the skills of people in disadvantaged areas to raise their productivity. Indeed, a key factor in understanding why some parts of Europe have successfully adapted to the digital revolution is their concentration of skilled workers that implement and invent new technologies that create entirely new types of products, services, or processes – in turn providing meaningful employment opportunities to millions of workers. Vast differences in skills exist within Europe, however, suggesting a potentially large scope for policy action. In particular, fostering skills that have become relatively more valuable over past decades – such as abstract reasoning, creativity, and complex problem-solving – should be a key priority for educational institutions and training providers.

To reduce the hardships and lack of opportunity facing individuals living in stagnating areas, easing intra-European migration and reducing barriers to housing construction in expanding regions are complementary policy levers. Higher mobility may serve to reduce regional differences in unemployment, by increasing the labour supply in areas with low unemployment and reducing it in areas with pervasive joblessness. Moreover, policymakers should ensure that the growth potential of already expanding city regions is not constrained by the supply of housing, which could serve as a drag on national growth.

Alternatively, governments may invest in stagnating places, trying to turn around and revive old manufacturing hubs in decline. However, evidence on the effectiveness of such policy interventions that often entail tax relief or employment subsidies is mixed at best. Rather than creating new jobs, place-based initiatives may instead shift economic activity from elsewhere; although some regions may benefit in relative terms, for the national economy it may be a zero-sum game. Against this background, such policies are unlikely to provide truly transformative change in regions in decline, since they fail to address the fact that a region's growth potential in the end reflects little more than the creativity and ingenuity of the people that live there.

DECENTRALISATION IN THE DIGITAL AGE

Digital technology provides unprecedented opportunities to decentralise decision-making processes to regional or metropolitan authorities, providing ways to engage citizens locally while also placing political power closer to the voter. Policymakers should work actively to exploit the open and decentralised nature of digital technology, which could be used to provide more efficient governance and service delivery. In 2014, nearly half of the population in the EU-28 interacted with public authorities via the internet, according to Eurostat. Yet, there is a scope for increased online interaction: in countries such as Italy and Poland, the share is a meager 23 per cent and 27 per cent respectively. An increased use of digital technology to tailor government services to different regional needs is one way to strike a balance between the efficiency gains from a centralised political system and the flexibility of decentralisation.

Regional or local authorities may also more effectively identify and engage with local stakeholders to provide solutions to unique regional challenges. A particularly appealing initiative, supported by the European commission, is the creation and support of digital competence centres that provide the local economy with expertise on digital technology, such as the Fraunhofer Institute in Germany and the Catapult centres in the UK. Facilitating access to new digital technologies, world-class digital experts and support to build bridges between local innovators, firms and customers throughout Europe could serve to substantially raise regional competitiveness. Local policymakers are further particularly well suited to identify the competitive advantages of a region, tailoring the services provided by such competence centres to match the specific requirements of the regional economy.

Yet, steps towards a more decentralised system may exacerbate regional inequalities as recent technological advances are projected to lead to the displacement of workers in a wider range of jobs. Recent estimates by Bruegel, a Belgian thinktank, suggest that nearly half of all European jobs could be automated in the next two decades. In particular, such disruption is likely to disproportionately affect regions that specialise in low-skill work that is becoming susceptible to automation. Against this background, a federal devolution may put increasing fiscal pressure on local governments to deal with costly retraining of displaced workers and rising unemployment. Striking a balance between decentralised decision-making that allows regions to adapt policies to local circumstances and strong central government support for disadvantaged regions should be at the centre of a progressive regional policy agenda.

OUTLOOK

Europe is currently undergoing a phase of rapid technological advancement as digital technologies increasingly permeate the workplace. Although technological advances have displaced workers in a wide range of routine work, digital technology remains a key source of job creation in Europe, with some 100,000 jobs created every year according to the European commission. Metropolitan regions that have been successful in transforming new technologies into new jobs are pulling ahead while others have seen jobs disappear, leading to regional decline. To bridge the growing regional divides, policies should be enacted that allow workers in struggling regions to develop the skills that are needed to transition into the jobs of the 21st century. In addition, regional authorities have an important role to play, in fostering multi-stakeholder partnerships that identify ways to promote skill development and job creation, to deliver growth in the digital age.

THE RISE OF THE CITIZEN EXPERT

Beth Simone Noveck

Does the EU need to be more democratic? It is not surprising that Jürgen Habermas, Europe's most famous democratic theorist, laments the dearth of mechanisms for "fulfilling the citizens' political will" in European institutions. The controversial handling of the Greek debt crisis, according to Habermas, was clear evidence of the need for more popular input into otherwise technocratic decision-making. Incremental progress toward participation does not excuse a growing crisis of democratic legitimacy that, he says, is undermining the European project.[1]

His complaints about European technocracy echo similar criticisms heard after the Dodd-Frank Wall Street Reform and Consumer Protection legislation enacted in the United States in 2010. To address the spectre of another 'too-big-to-fail' financial firm collapse like Lehman Brothers, the legislation created an elite Financial Stability Oversight Council comprised of heads of major financial regulatory agencies accountable only to Congress through an annual report.

For participatory democrats like Habermas, opportunities for deliberative democratic input by citizens are essential to legitimacy. And, to be sure, the absence of such opportunities is no guarantee of more effective outcomes. A Greek referendum in July 2015 scuttled European austerity plans.

But pitting technocracy against citizenship is a false dichotomy resulting from the long-held belief, even among reformers, that only professional public servants or credentialed elites possess the requisite abilities to govern in a complex society. Citizens are spectators who can express opinions but cognitive incapacity, laziness or simply the complexity of modern society limit participation to asking people what they feel by means of elections, opinion polls, or social media.

Although seeing technocracy as the antinomy of citizenship made sense when expertise was difficult to pinpoint, now tools like LinkedIn, which make knowhow more searchable, are making it possible for public institutions to get more help from more diverse sources – including from within the civil service – systematically and could enable more members of the public to participate actively in governing based on what they know and care about. It is high time for institutions to begin to leverage such platforms to match the need for expertise to the demand for it and, in the process, increase engagement becoming more effective and more legitimate.

Such software does more than catalogue credentials. The internet is radically decreasing the costs of identifying diverse forms of expertise so that the person who has taken courses on an online learning platform can showcase those credentials with a searchable digital badge. The person who has answered thousands of questions on a question-and-answer website can demonstrate their practical ability and willingness to help. Ratings by other users further attest to the usefulness of their contributions. In short, it is becoming possible to discover what people know and can do in ever more finely tuned ways and match people to opportunities to participate that speak to their talents.

MATCHING DEMAND TO SUPPLY OF EXPERTISE

Governments routinely turn to the public for help off and online. The European Food Safety Authority, for example, is trying to crowdsource better expertise to address food-borne illness.[2] Since its inception in 2010, federal American agencies have run more than 450 challenges via Challenge.gov, which showcases requests by government agencies to the public to tackle hard problems in exchange for cash prizes and other incentives.

Yet as appealing as an open call might be for tapping into the ideas of smart and willing citizens, it will never transform how we govern. That is because this typical crowdsourcing method fails to match individuals to what matters to them or, in this case, match people to problems based on what they can do.

To make all forms of engagement more effective, we need to increase the likelihood that the opportunity to participate will be known to those who need to participate. If a city really wants to improve the chances of crafting a workable plan for bike lanes, it should be able to reach out to urban planners, transportation engineers, cyclists, and cab drivers and offer them ways to participate meaningfully. When a public organisation needs hands on help from techies to build better websites or data crunching from data scientists, it needs to be able to connect.

Already an accelerating practice in the private sector, where managers want to increase the likelihood of finding employees with the right skills, something they cannot do easily from transcripts alone, public institutions are beginning to try matching the supply to the demand for expertise. This year the World Bank created its own expert network called SkillFinder to index the talents of its 27,000 employees, consultants and alumni. With the launch of SkillFinder, the bank is just beginning to explore how to organise its human capital to achieve the bank's mission of eradicating poverty.

In the United States, there are early efforts to help civil servants better target expertise among their colleagues at the rank-and-file level. HHS Profiles is a project designed to help the Department of Health and Human Services more quickly find employees, for example, to staff medical device safety review panels.[3]

Giving people outside as well as inside institutions opportunities to share their knowledge could save time, financial resources and even lives. Take the example of PulsePoint, a smartphone app created by the fire department of San Ramon, California. Now used by 1400 communities across the United States, PulsePoint matches those with a specific skill, namely CPR training, with dramatic results. By tapping into a feed of the 911 calls, PulsePoint sends a text message "CPR Needed!" to those registered members of the public near the victim. Effective bystander CPR immediately administered can potentially double or triple the victim's chance of survival. By augmenting traditional government first response, PulsePoint's matching has already helped over 7,000 victims.

As Mark Wilson, neurosurgeon and co-founder of GoodSAM – a UK service similar to PulsePoint but that targets off-duty doctors, nurses and police officers – wrote in an email: "Using the same analogy that you are never more than five metres from a spider, we figured in cities you're probably never more than 200m from a doctor, nurse, paramedic or someone able to hold an airway and (if appropriate) perform high quality CPR. The problem was alerting these people to nearby emergencies".

Such targeting is an invigoration of the opportunity to participate in the life of our democracy beyond going to the ballot box once a year. It deepens and redefines citizenship. When a person comes to the aid of an accident victim they are participating in governance, even if only in a small way. This has nothing to do with support for partisan causes or candidates. It has everything to do with what it means to be a citizen in a contemporary democracy.

In an era in which it is commonplace for companies to use technology to segment customers in an effort to promote their products more effectively, the idea of matching might sound obvious. To be sure, it is common practice in business – but in the public sphere, the notion that participation should be tailored to the individual's abilities and tethered to day-to-day practices of governing, not politicking, is new. More accurately, it is a revival of Athenian life where citizen competence and expertise were central to economic and military success.

What makes this kind of targeted engagement truly democratic – and citizenship in this vision more active, robust, and meaningful –

is that such targeting allows us to multiply the number and frequency of ways to engage productively in a manner consistent with each person's talents. When we move away from focusing on citizen opinion to discovering citizen expertise, we catalyse participation that is also independent of geographical boundaries.

TAKING CITIZEN EXPERTISE SERIOUSLY: POLICY RECOMMENDATIONS

The first step to creating what Susan Moffitt calls "participatory bureaucracy" is the clear and repeated articulation by world leaders, public intellectuals, activists, and bloggers of the core idea: the imperative to take the capacity and expertise of citizens seriously and to put it to use in service of our democracy.

Given how radical a departure these participatory ways of working are from the closed-door status quo (or the view that participation is limited to voting and opinion polling), we cannot declare, define, and repeat often enough what it could mean to embrace collaboration and co-creation; to make consultation part of operations on a day-to-day basis; to strive for constant conversation with an engaged and knowledgeable public and to reinvent the conception of public service and of the public servant as the steward of such a conversation.

Second, policymakers need to create or update the legal frameworks that dictate how governments get expertise using new technology. The norm in both Europe and the United States is the formation of small committees that meet in person a few times a year and produce a report but cannot avail themselves of new technology to ask questions on a more frequent basis of more distributed experts.

Third, more tech companies also need to build a wider variety of matching tools to tap talent, especially talent within the public service, reliably in the public interest. Bill and Melinda Gates, for example, committed to support the creation of a global database of citizen skills. NovaGob and JoinUp are both trying to use technology to help public professionals learn from one another.

Just as King Henry II invented the jury in the 12th century and thus handed power to citizens in a practical and transformative fashion, we are at the threshold of being able to create these new institutional mechanisms. But that will require going beyond principles and pronouncements to create the expert networking and collaboration platforms that make it possible in practice.

Fourth, changing how we make decisions will depend squarely on having the personnel who embrace openness and collaboration. The recognition of citizen expertise does not mean jettisoning the professionals – far from it. The new civil servant will be able to coordinate multiple channels for dialogue, viewing these processes as core, and not incidental, to the job. The demand for leaders of such conversational organisations should create pressure for new curricula and training to meet the need.

Fifth, private sector employers can accelerate the ability to target expertise and accelerate more participatory governing by going beyond merely asking employees for HR information and, instead, begin to catalogue systematically the unique skills of the individuals within their organisation into public-facing talent banks. Many employers are anyway turning to new technology to match employees (and would-be employees) with the right skills to available jobs. How easily they could develop and share databases with public information about who has what experience while at the same time protecting the privacy of personal information.

CONSEQUENCES OF THE FAILURE TO INNOVATE

These technologies of expertise make it possible to go beyond the proxies of expertise like credentials or professional membership, which have led to attenuated forms of advising and a resulting distrust of experts and the governments they serve. They point to a future in which it is possible – in concrete, actionable fashion – to unlock expertise within government; credentialed expertise and non-traditional forms of distributed know-how outside of government. Although in many places, we enjoy well-functioning government institutions run by competent professionals, the failure to take advantage of new data-rich tools to enable government to reliably get expertise – credentialed, skilled and experiential – imposes a significant opportunity cost. The greatest challenge of our time is to create political institutions innovative enough to tackle increasingly complex issues from ensuring economic stability to stopping terrorism to saving the planet. Closed-door ways of working rob us of the innovative ideas, robust talents, hard work, and diverse perspectives that are vital to making government more effective.

NOTES

1. Habermas, J. (2015) *The Lure of Technocracy*. Cambridge: Polity Press; see also Waldron, J. (2015) 'The Vanishing Europe of Jürgen Habermas', in: *The New York Review of Books*, 22 October, pp. 70–72.

2. European Food Safety Authority (2015) 'Crowdsourcing: Engaging communities effectively in food and feed risk assessment', *ESFA website*, http://www.efsa.europa.eu/en/tenders/tender/ocefsaamu201503.

3. Hernandez, J. & Rosamilia, N. (2015) 'Developing a model for expert networking across federal government: The HHS profile pilot', *Figshare*, https://figshare.com/articles/Developing_a_Model_for_Expert_Networking_Across_Federal_Government_The_HHS_Profiles_Pilot/2002110.

Part III

Social Policy: Upskilling and Social Investment

PREVENTATIVE POLICY IN ACTION – NORTH RHINE-WESTPHALIA

Hannelore Kraft

"**A**n ounce of prevention is worth a pound of cure". Almost 300 years later, this proverbial insight by Benjamin Franklin has lost none of its pertinence. On the contrary: in the state of North Rhine-Westphalia we want to show not only that preventative policy pays off in Benjamin Franklin's sense, but that prevention can help us to avoid social follow-up costs.

Germany is one of the European countries marked by a very low birth rate and a rapidly ageing population. As the ratio of children and young people in the total population declines, the need for government support grows in proportion. In North Rhine-Westphalia (NRW – see box), for example, the number of parents who are overwhelmed by the task of child-raising and whose children thus must be taken into state custody rose by over 30 per cent between 2006 and 2010. That is to say: although we have fewer young people, they are nonetheless increasingly dependent on state-sponsored child-raising assistance.

This trend entails enormous costs for the welfare state. When I became premier of North Rhine-Westphalia in 2010, one of our first measures was to commission a study to find answers to the question: how much money do we spend here in our state to "repair" things that have gone wrong in the social realm. Money that is needed, for example, to assist young people who do not finish school in finding some sort of gainful employment.

North Rhine-Westphalia

- Largest German state with a population of 17.6 million
- Industrial centre with 19 of the 50 largest German companies
- Would rank 19th as an independent nation among the world's major economies

The study found that the social follow-up costs run to €23.6bn per year! €23.6bn that are either incurred as direct costs by the municipal, state and federal governments and the social insurance agencies, or which they are then missing in taxes and duties.

"LEAVE NO CHILD BEHIND!" – "EVERY CHILD MATTERS"

If we want to reduce social follow-up costs, it is time to shift our perspective and to rethink our social democracy. We want to transform the welfare state which usually focuses on repairing damage into a state that invests early on in children and education so that consequential social costs are avoided in the first place.

The state government of North Rhine-Westphalia has embraced precisely this change in perspective. Under the motto "Leave No Child Behind!" it has formulated a policy approach that sees prevention as a mission cutting across all functional departments and administration levels, with the aim of enabling every child to grow up to become a successful adult.

The earlier we foster children's development, the more likely they are to grow up healthy and to succeed in their education. They will presumably become well-integrated members of society and be less dependent on social assistance. But investments in prevention avoid more than just social costs. A growing number of scientific studies demonstrate that they also bring a substantial return.

PREVENTION PAYS OFF

Arguably the most famous among these studies is the Perry Preschool Project, named after a preschool in a small town in the US state of Michigan. In the early 1960s a group of around 120 children there were admitted to a special pre-primary programme. A long-term study was set up to follow and analyse how these children's lives developed.

The study found that children who received this extra support with learning early on developed better in practically every way than a control group. They earned higher degrees, got better jobs, were healthier, and came into conflict with the law less frequently.

One person who took a great interest in the Perry Preschool Project was James Heckman, an American economist and Nobel laureate in economics in 2000. Heckman undertook an attempt to calculate the economic dimension of the preschool programme. His conclusion: society benefitted greatly.

Converted to the value of the dollar in the year 2000, the costs for the preschool programme came to around $15,000 per participant. But because the sponsored children cost society less in the following four decades, society "earned" so to speak an average of nearly $260,000 for each child.

It is hard to imagine a better investment. Or, in the words of James Heckman: "It pays off seven to 10 per cent per annum for each dollar invested. The stock market between 1945 and 2008 was a six or seven per cent return".

LOCAL PREVENTION CHAINS: CRADLE TO CAREER

North Rhine-Westphalia is implementing preventative policy with a strategy that pursues two main objectives: first, developing so-called "prevention chains", and secondly, strengthening the state-wide prevention infrastructure.

Preventative policy must begin where children live and grow up. A key role is therefore played by the municipalities, because in the German federal system they have the main authority for shaping the living environments of children and families.

Together with the Bertelsmann Foundation, we launched the pilot project "Leave No Child Behind! Municipalities in NRW take preventative action" in early 2012. The project involves supporting 18 towns and districts with a total of almost 5 million inhabitants in developing "local prevention chains". Like the links in a chain, all the relevant local stakeholders and programmes are to be linked up in order to guide and support children and families. They set out to initiate collaborations between child, youth and family welfare agencies, health services, schools and education services, culture, sport and other leisure organisations, training agencies and employment services, the police and courts. Our prevention chain focuses on each child's life journey. It already begins with the mother's pregnancy and extends to successful entry into the career world – hence "from cradle to career".

STRENGTHENING STATE-WIDE PREVENTION INFRASTRUCTURE

Similar to the local prevention chains, we are also building a comprehensive prevention infrastructure at the state level. We are thus investing – among other things – in children and education.

Special priority is given to expanding early childhood support. Ten years ago, daycare was practically unavailable for children under three years of age. Today, half of all children aged one to two years can be looked after at a daycare centre or by a childminder.

Schooling is another example. Ten years ago, half-day schools were still the rule in Germany. Today, four out of 10 pupils in North Rhine-Westphalia attend all-day schooling, which is offered in a flexible mix of obligatory and voluntary forms.

INTERIM RESULTS

What have we achieved thus far? We did a first interim stocktaking of our pilot project "Leave No Child Behind!" in the summer of 2014. The results show that prevention works.

One example is a pilot project in the town of Arnsberg (population 73,000). Here we have succeeded in a socially problematic neighbourhood in reducing the proportion of preschool children with language problems by 20 per cent since 2010. At the same time, almost twice as many children now attend a secondary school leading to the *Abitur* qualification for university studies. And in the past five years, no child under 14 years of age had to be taken into state custody.

Another example is the town of Hamm (population 175,000), which is implementing a programme of individual support for schoolchildren within the scope of "Leave No Child Behind!" After only one and a half years, truancy has been cut by 50 per cent. And just under 95 per cent of the pupils receiving support have attained a higher school-leaving certificate as a result.

A third example, which also illustrates the fiscal effects of our preventative policy, comes from Bielefeld (population 325,000). Through various preventative measures, the number of those receiving child-raising assistance in Bielefeld was reduced between 2010 and 2013 by nearly five per cent (4.6 per cent) – saving the town budget €2.2m.

The positive effects of the improved prevention infrastructure can also be felt at the state level. The additional places in daycare centres and all-day schools, for example, are not only good for the children's development. They also help parents to achieve a better work-life balance. The number of mothers of underage children able to pursue gainful employment thus increased from 2007 to 2012 by an estimated 60,000. Each working mother represents added value of some €63,500 per year. That is to say: these additional working mothers have led to an increase in the gross domestic product of North Rhine-Westphalia by €3.7bn.

Our first experiences in North Rhine-Westphalia with a policy of prevention are quite promising. It seems possible through preventative measures to already realise measurable savings in social follow-up costs in the short to medium term. However, there is still much to do. Prevention is after all an ambitious, long-term policy project, the full benefits of which will not be seen during a short term in office but only in the course of a generation.

THE CHANGING NATURE OF JOBS – AND A POLICY AGENDA ON EDUCATION AND TRAINING FOR HIGH-VALUE JOBS

Lodewijk Asscher

As a parent of three young children, I have often appreciated drawings of a tadpole figure, brought home from school. This endearing sketch represents a human being, whose arms and legs are growing straight out of his head, because his body has been playfully and conveniently omitted. All children draw human beings by this typical formula; it is how they see the world.

As a representation of society, the tadpole metaphor is not endearing and harmless. On the contrary, it shows us as a society from which the core, a strong middle class that typically binds the upper and lower echelons, has disappeared. Unfortunately – unlike my children's drawings – the tadpole society is becoming ever more realistic, especially now that technology is advancing and the age of the robots is dawning.

Although we do not know precisely what the future will bring us, it is a bad idea to wait and see what happens. We need to craft a new progressive agenda as quickly as possible that is both stout and flexible enough to face the uncertain future that awaits us.

THE AGE OF THE ROBOTS

Robots are becoming more accessible, reliable and affordable. Compared to humans, they are cheaper, faster, never get sick and work

24 hours a day. They also never ask for pay rises, do not belong to trade unions and do not go on strike. They have the potential to replace employees in many existing jobs, particularly middle-income positions. Computers are already faster and more efficient than humans when it comes to the handling of administrative and repetitive work tasks. For this reason, jobs in administration are decreasing.[1]

The advent of artificial intelligence, big data, faster internet connections and the smartphone open up an even greater range of new applications. Robots could soon become cleaners, warehouse workers and taxi drivers.

Perhaps this still sounds like pie in the sky to you. Yet we should not underestimate the current pace of technological development. The scholars Erik Brynjolfsson and Andrew McAfee illustrate the power of exponential development in a seminal book, in which they argue that exponential growth goes relatively unnoticed for some time, and suddenly explodes into view.[2] Digital development has now reached this point, expanding at an incredible rate and with its far-reaching effects now becoming evidently clear. In their own much-discussed publication, Carl Frey and Michael Osborne conclude that, due to technology, almost half of the jobs in the United States are at risk of disappearing in the coming two decades.[3]

OPPORTUNITY AS A LUXURY ITEM

After the second world war, our accumulated wealth was more or less equally shared, providing opportunities for most people. From the 1990s onwards, however, income from work as a percentage of total wealth started to fall in comparison to income from capital. In developed countries, the labour share – wages as a percentage of national income – has fallen from 66 per cent to 62 per cent.[4] At the same time, the share of the one per cent best-paid employees increased by 20 per cent.[5] Even in more egalitarian societies like Germany, Denmark and Sweden, the gap between the richest 10 per cent and the poorest 10 per cent is widening. Owners of capital and the highest earners are benefiting most, with ordinary workers getting a smaller slice of the cake.[6]

These trends mean that the wages of the average worker are lagging behind. Between 1999 and 2011, productivity grew twice as much as the average wage.[7] Employees' income security is also decreasing. In almost all developed countries the percentage of flexible workers is increasing, at the ever-increasing expense of permanent employees.[8] Wage differentials between employees with different levels of education are also increasing. In 1995, a Dutch employee with a university education earned 37 per cent more than someone with a secondary vocational education. By 2009, this had risen to more than 50 per cent.[9]

In the age of the robots, inequality may spread further. It is likely that companies will switch to new technologies en masse and their productivity will rise sharply. Yet the majority of the wealth this would generate would end up in the hands of the people who own the robots. Of course, highly qualified employees would also benefit, as their skills are required to ensure that the robots operate correctly. Yet middle-income earners and those at the bottom would lose out. This could lead to the real threat of prolonged technological unemployment.

Already, robots have eroded job security and income for some groups in the labour markets. Previously, the impact of technology was confined to low-skilled jobs, but now the middle class is really feeling the impact too.[10] As a result of globalisation, 'flexibilisation' and recently 'robotisation', a squeezed middle class is threatened by migrant workers who are willing to work for less, by highly educated people working below their level, and by technology making jobs obsolete. For these people, the pathways to a better life are being barricaded one by one. Education is no longer a prerequisite for success, nor is hard work. Opportunity is becoming a luxury item only available to the well-connected few.

THE POWER OF THE MIDDLE CLASS

A recent report by the Netherlands Institute for Social Research stated that dealing with structural inequality is an urgent task for policymakers – especially when the social divide is still bridgeable.[11]

Unfortunately, rightwingers urge us forward in a race to the bottom, while claiming that the left is as scared of robots as their forebears were of steam engines.

It is a cheap trick aimed at directing attention away from the real issue at stake. Indeed, it is not about whether we should choose for robots or for people, or whether or not we should stick to the past: it is about moulding the future in the way we want it to be. Under the right circumstances, people and robots are perfectly complimentary to one another.

Yet we need to create these circumstances. The fact is we cannot afford our middle class to dissipate. Historically, a strong middle class has always been our society's tower of strength, the vital sinew for solidarity, emancipation and equal opportunities. The middle class offers those in the lower echelons of society a perspective to move up in life. It is of the utmost importance to strengthen our middle class and prevent the social divide from increasing, in particular now that the age of the robots is dawning.

EMBRACING INNOVATION

Innovation is not a fate that befalls us, but an opportunity we need to embrace on our own terms.

First, we should invest in human capital (social innovation) rather than just in technology. We are far too busy with the question of 'what will robots bring us' that we tend to forget about upgrading human skills.

Education is a crucial factor. We are finding ourselves in a race between education and technology, as the economist Jan Tinbergen predicted years ago. We have to invest in education and stimulate students to complete their higher education. This can be done by offering individual learning paths and the possibility of online education so people can combine their studies with work and family responsibilities.

It is also important to make our education system future-proof, enabling us to acquire the right skills for the future. Robots are already better than humans in performing many routine tasks. Yet we can make a difference with our creativity, negotiation, communication and analytical skills. Workers can acquire the relevant skills if we invest in our education system. We should not be afraid to make the necessary changes. Only by stimulating informal learning, developing more flexible education, and customising curricula, can we build a responsive society that can cope with future challenges.

Innovation should involve more than just technological advances. Between 60 and 80 per cent of successful innovation is determined by social innovation. If companies only invest in technological innovation, employment will decrease by 5.8 per cent, as employees are unable to apply the new technology. Yet if companies also invest in social innovation, employment increases by 8.3 per cent on average. By investing in employees, collaborating and tapping into new knowledge together, we are embracing innovation in a way that allows everyone to profit from it.

Second, embracing innovation means that we should invest in the types of innovation that we want. Technology has the potential to solve the world problems and truly help mankind. They can perform dangerous and arduous tasks, ranging from the dismantling of bombs to laying paving slabs. By investing in entrepreneurship, we can create a fertile breeding ground for this type of innovation. Europe is full of young entrepreneurs with creative, fresh ideas. The number of startups in the Netherlands is growing fast and some of them have already become major companies, such as Adyen, Coolblue and WetTansfer. Also, an increasing number of foreign investors want to invest in Dutch startups. It is now important that the startups expand themselves, so that they can employ more people.

Lastly, embracing technology means that we take the lead in creating a labour market of our choice, instead of letting technology take control. This means anticipating future challenges, as technological developments are bound to have an impact on our labour market as a whole, potentially leading to unemployment and income security.

We need advanced labour market reform. By this I mean the radical decision to opt for higher productivity rather than cheaper labour.

We should opt for work security rather than job security. In addition, we should opt for the right to training as a fundamental right for workers, but also a fundamental duty. I want to explore the option to earmark a fixed share of the payroll for vocational training. The Netherlands is already preparing itself for a better future. With regard to employment-protection legislation and unemployment benefits, current reforms introduce work-to-work transitions and the transition allowance, which unemployed people can use to finance training. It will help them in finding another job in another sector and it also strengthens incentives to pick up work.

It is important to stimulate work-to-work transitions (job mobility) even more, as it strengthens the labour market position of workers. It should be easier to start a second career during your working life, for example by creating life-course savings schemes that can fund training during your career or by introducing educational loan systems for adults. Changing your career path in time can prevent unemployment.

At the same time we have to take care of the social consequences of technological development. What does the rise of the robots imply for our income distribution and job security? Extreme inequality is undesirable and harms economic growth. In the long run, a fair division of welfare is a key ingredient for an inclusive society with opportunities for all. This can only be accomplished by redistribution of wealth.

If you believe the globalists, opportunity is a self-managing unit that will sort itself out along the way. Everyone will get their fair share – and if you did not get yours, then you must have done something terribly wrong. This is of course contentious logic. Opportunity is not a guaranteed fait accompli, but a political choice regarding the redistribution of wealth. It is like shuffling the cards before a poker match. Redistribution ensures everyone gets a fair deal; an equal opportunity of winning the game.

It is very easy to respond reflexively and rashly to technological advances, either by simplistically seeing robots as money-makers that will bring us lots of cash, or by seeing them as intruders that we should keep out. Such Pavlovian reactions will only soothe short-term worries and desires. It is okay to smell the opportunities, but let us not be blind to the drawbacks. It is time to develop as swiftly as possible a progressive agenda that crosses national borders, as well as the borders between government and social partners. Progressives need to unite themselves against the neoliberal forces that are pulling Europe into a race to the bottom, while bartering the value of work away in the marketplace. Only by teaming up can we preserve the precious social attainments that we have fought so hard for in the past decades. We need to introduce and commit ourselves to a 'robot directive' – a package of measures regarding redistribution, education, social innovation, and advanced labour market reform. Together, we need to make the employment of low-skilled workers cheaper, prevent tax evasion by multinationals, and reinject the profits of these big companies back into society. Only then can we reap the benefits of technology and robotisation on our own terms, while ensuring that opportunity remains a luxury everyone can afford. In the future of our choice, there is no room for a tadpole society.

NOTES

1. David, H. (2015) 'Why are There Still so Many Jobs? The History and Future of Workplace Automation', *Journal of Economic Perspectives,* 29(3), pp. 3–30, https://www.aeaweb.org/articles.php?doi=10.1257/jep.29.3.3.
2. Brynjolfsson, E. & McAfee, A. (2014) *The Second Machine Age: Work, progress, and Prosperity in a Time of Brilliant Technologies,* New York: W. W. Norton & Company, http://books.wwnorton.com/books/The-Second-Machine-Age/.
3. Frey, C. B. & Osborne. M. A. (2013) 'The Future of Employment: How Susceptible are Jobs to Computerisation?', *Oxford Martin School,* http://www.oxfordmartin.ox.ac.uk/downloads/academic/The_Future_of_Employment.pdf.
4. Organisation for Economic Co-operation and Development.
5. Organisation for Economic Co-operation and Development (2011) 'Divided We Stand: Why Inequality Keeps Rising', http://www.

oecd-ilibrary.org/social-issues-migration-health/the-causes-of-growing-inequalities-in-oecd-countries_9789264119536-en.

6. Organisation for Economic Co-operation and Development (2011) 'Divided We Stand: Why Inequality Keeps Rising', http://www.oecd-ilibrary.org/social-issues-migration-health/the-causes-of-growing-inequalities-in-oecd-countries_9789264119536-en.

7. International Labour Organisation.

8. Organisation for Economic Co-operation and Development.

9. ter Weel, B. (2012) 'Wage Inequality is Rising in Netherlands', *CPB Economische beleidsanalyse*, http://www.cpb.nl/publicatie/loonongelijkheid-nederland-stijgt.

10. Maarten, G., Manning, A. & Salomons, A. (2009) 'Job Polarisation in Europe', *American Economic Review*, 99(2), pp. 58–63, https://www.aeaweb.org/articles.php?doi=10.1257/aer.99.2.58.

11. Vrooman, C., Gijsbert, M. & Boelhouwer, J. (2014) *Difference in Netherlands*, http://www.scp.nl/Publicaties/Alle_publicaties/Publicaties_2014/Verschil_in_Nederland.

TRAINING AND PROTECTING IN THE INNOVATING ECONOMY

Pierre-Yves Geoffard

Like any period rich in innovation, the 'digital revolution' generates both hope and fear. There is hope for new opportunities: new jobs emerge, more productive technologies create more wealth through less work, and the use of intelligent machines relinquishes people of physical work. As well, more mutually beneficial exchanges are possible through a better flow of information. However, there is great fear of threats to many too: skills once valuable have now become obsolete; jobs which are created are structurally precarious; and the benefits of innovation remain concentrated within a few without benefiting all, subsequently increasing inequalities and threatening the cohesion of society.

So how can we limit or offset the negative consequences of digital innovation to unlock the potential created by these new technologies? In at least three areas, our societies must evolve profoundly: education, social protection, wealth redistribution.

Digital technologies penetrate all sectors of the economy, and deeply affect the organisation of our society; sometimes this is gradual, sometimes it is sudden. The smooth and fast flow of information that is distinctive for the 'digital revolution' is primarily a phenomenon of generalised disintermediation. The most striking examples of this are well known: AirBnB puts owners of homes in direct contact with potential tenants, eBay connects sellers and buyers, Uber links car owners and those wishing to be transported, etc. Previously, these relations were based on intermediate structures whose function was to collect relevant information, both on the supply and demand for these services. Therefore, perhaps less spectacular but equally important; the removal of intermediate levels lead to the formation of companies that are less hierarchical and slimmer than the large industrial enterprises that emerged during the industrial revolution. Middle management loses importance and is seen to be directly threatened by the direct flow of information between different individuals or entities making up a business.

The recent works of Ariel Reshef, James Harrigan and Farid Toubal[1] indicate that the destruction of intermediate jobs is especially prevalent in the top technology companies. It seems that the digitalisation of the economy renders employment obsolete for those whose tasks, manual or intellectual, has a rather repetitive nature; these jobs have also long been the preserve of the middle classes. Many countries experience a fragmentation or 'dualisation' of their labour markets: jobs created are both very skilled and well paid, or they are at the bottom of the ladder, insecure and poorly paid. This disappearance of intermediate jobs through information technology bypasses the core function of middle-income jobs, putting the richest and poorest in relation with one another.

Beyond these effects of disintermediation, many digital innovations make it possible to perform a set of tasks consisting of intellectual, but sometimes repetitive, content (accounting, back office, etc) automatically. The danger lies in the eradication of intellectual activities processing and synthesising information, tasks which can now be assigned machinery capable of handling infinitely large amounts of data that the human brain cannot grasp. So it is not only low-skilled workers, whose tasks can be performed by machines, which are under threat, but also many service trades too. The overall result is that many intermediate occupations, traditionally held by middle class workers, are directly threatened by digital innovations, which has made them more efficient with the help of 'machines', of 'robots' or 'algorithms'.

These fears are legitimate in part. Innovation has certainly destroyed existing jobs, but the effect on total employment and unemployment that digital innovation has is not necessarily negative. Everything depends on social and political responses made to the challenges posed by changing technologies.

The first positive effect of innovation on employment is well known and often mentioned: if machines make certain human activities obsolete, we must also have a need to design, build, and manage these machines. This innovative destruction creates new, highly skilled business. Consequently, we need fewer workers but more engineers. So the first benefit of technological innovation is that it leads to productivity gains, and allows us to produce equal amounts of goods with less human labour. However, it is illusory and absurd to expect that these new jobs will be as numerous as those that are destroyed. This net job destruction has always been the effect of innovation, and this effect is profoundly beneficial: it is nothing but the only long-term engine of progress of human societies that entrusts more and more tasks to machines clearing people's time, free to focus on other, often more rewarding, activities. The invention of the washing machine has destroyed the jobs of thousands, even millions, of washerwomen, but the spread of this technology has meant that hundreds of millions of people do not have to devote many hours each day to household laundry.

The second effect of innovation is macroeconomic, less immediate and less guaranteed. Gains in productivity and more skilled jobs result in increased revenues. These income gains translate into increased consumption and therefore demand for many goods and services whose production requires labour: as a result, employment may increase. However, this looping effect is not mechanical. Because income from increased productivity benefits primarily the holders of capital, be it physical capital (for instance the owners of machines) or human capital (highly skilled workers who design or operate machinery).

Moreover, the most visible innovations include digital direct linking platforms of individuals to different situations but may engage in a mutually beneficial exchange. These platforms are strongly increasing returns to scale, and often have all the characteristics of a natural monopoly; even more than in traditional sectors of the economy, digital innovation is conducive to the phenomenon of the 'winner takes all' mentality grounded in the unprecedented speed of formation of considerable fortunes for a few individuals who had the right idea at the right time, and have been able to put this idea into practice.

But if the 'winners of innovation' are already rich or very rich, they spend their income gains to savings more than consumption, reinforcing the concentration of wealth without feeding new jobs. Certainly, they can also, as in any highly unequal society, appeal to many domestic services. But the prospect of a polarised world where the general population works in order to make the lives of a few Bill Gates or Mark Zuckerbergs more comfortable may not be more encouraging.

We see that technological innovation benefits all, yet two things are needed: first, that enough workers are ready to perform the jobs created by new technologies; and second, that income gains are sufficiently divided, which is important both in terms of social justice but also to indirectly feed a demand for goods and services resulting in job creation.

If the number of workers trained in more skilled jobs is not increasing at the same rate as corporate demand for this type of work, innovation will result in a strong polarisation of wages. The Dutch economist Jan Tinbergen has identified the importance of this 'race between technology and training' as a powerful factor in increasing inequality. The only way to meet this danger is to invest heavily in education: they must be trained for future trades.

But what are the jobs of tomorrow or after tomorrow, in societies where workers will also have life-long careers? Nobody knows. The only certainty is that it will, throughout people's careers, form new businesses and that more time should be devoted to it. Unless you accept that technological evolution leaves whole battalions of workers 'on the tile', educational systems must be adapted to match the needs of people's life-long careers. In the future, initial training should prepare young people, not just for business today, not even the jobs of tomorrow, but for the training of tomorrow that allows them to constantly adapt their skills to an ever-changing job world, which in turn will prepare for careers after tomorrow.

The fight against the forces that, through innovation, lead to an increase in inequality is also necessary. Redistributive tax policies – taxing human or physical capital – have a crucial role to play in preventing such abuses. But such policies are themselves threatened by freer movement of capital, including financial, through the country. With the fight against tax havens, increased coordination of fiscal policies across Europe seems to be a minimum requirement in order to avoid tax competition between countries. As a result, this process has led to taxing less mobile production factors, ie the less skilled labour, producing deleterious effects on employment and incomes of these categories of workers.

The changes in work itself deserve our attention too. Not only will the jobs of tomorrow not be the same as those destroyed by new technologies, but the form itself may be very different, much more flexible but also more precarious. The role of platforms for the rapid exchange of real-time information on supply and demand for services is also crucial. The most striking example is urban transport: demand is structurally fluctuating, greatly challenging its levels of permanent supply. The flow of information allows workers to quickly determine and locate the upsurge of potential demand. The type of job created is precarious and uncertain, but allows individuals excluded from the 'traditional' labour market to take advantage of new opportunities for rewarding employment;[2] how then should companies be organised to allow these jobs to exist, while protecting workers who are engaged in such activity?

In many countries, the protection mechanisms against the major risks of life – unemployment, retirement, family or illness – are based on architecture that dates back to a period of high growth, full employment (male), and stable family structures. As the social rights were attached to the stable, full-time employment position of the householder, all family members used to be covered against risks. These models do not respond well to increased job insecurity. Today, job loss is often losing access to social protection, which adds to the precarious insecurity, and makes the effects of unemployment even more dramatic. We need to rethink social protection in depth: it is individuals who need to be covered against these risks, regardless of their activity, employed or not. Moreover, even if not directly from social protection, access to housing can also be weakened by the absence of regular income and stable characteristic of wage labour.

Digital innovation raises a crucial question with respect to social issues: should we protect the past from the future, or the future from the past? Preparing workers for the future means greatly increasing the training efforts of individuals but also enabling those who lose their jobs to not suddenly lose the social rights associated with that job. It is necessary to enable them to do everything they can to take advantage of opportunities and activities kicked off by new technologies, and to adapt social protection so that it specifically protects workers engaged in precarious work.

NOTES

1. James H., Ariell R. & Farid T. (2015) 'The March of the Techies: Technology, Trade, and Job Polarization in France, 1994–2007', http://people.virginia.edu/~ar7kf/papers/Harrigan_Reshef_Toubal_September_2015.pdf.

2. The registration data of drivers VTC show that they are particularly concentrated in areas with high unemployment, low education level, and low wages. http://variationseconomiques.net/tag/vtc/.

A MODERN AND FAIR LABOUR MARKET AGENDA FOR EUROPE

Enrique Fernández-Macías

A modern labour market agenda in Europe should try to boost job creation by following the high-road model of Nordic economies, rather than the employment flexibilisation strategy that has been dominant in recent years. Such an agenda should also openly confront the socioeconomic divergence effect of the Economic and Monetary Union (EMU), by coordinating employment policies and fostering EU-level redistribution mechanisms. And it should initiate a serious debate about how to reorganise our socioeconomic systems if, as seems increasingly plausible, there is a generalised substitution of human labour by robots in a not so distant future.

What elements should be part of a modern labour market agenda in the EU? I would like to concentrate on three challenges (two of immediate application, one more speculative) that are facing European labour markets, and discuss some ideas on what can be done about them.

CHALLENGE ONE: TO CONFRONT JOB POLARISATION AND DE-STANDARDISATION, FOLLOW THE NORDIC MODEL

In many European countries, employment growth has been anaemic since the 1980s, with high levels of unemployment becoming endemic. The preferred approach to confront this problem has been to make employment relations less regulated and more flexible. In some cases (though not all), this resulted in faster employment creation – but often at the expense of job quality and economic stability. For instance, the deregulation of employment contracts in Spain in the 1980s led to a massive expansion of temporary employment (up to a third of all employment contracts in Spain): however, this resulted in a brutal segmentation of the labour market, a big expansion of low-value-added activities and jobs, and a more unstable economy due to the fast turnover of temporary employment contracts.

The current success of the German economy may have shaky foundations for similar reasons: successive rounds of labour market deregulation have reduced unemployment to a very low level, but at the expense of a very significant expansion of jobs in low-value-added activities, with very precarious conditions. As a result, Germany has become the canonic case of job polarisation in Europe since the 1980s[1] and has increased its share of low-paid employment to the highest level in Europe (in 2010, the share of workers with wages below 60 per cent of the median in Germany was 24 per cent).[2]

So what can be done? Our own research[3] shows that, although de-standardisation and job polarisation have generally grown across Europe, there are very significant exceptions that prove that such polarisation is by no means inescapable. In the last few decades, the small Nordic economies have managed to maintain low levels of unemployment while expanding high value economic activities and creating mostly high quality jobs. Sweden is a paradigmatic case: since the 1970s, it has been consistently shifting employment from low to high skilled occupations, without a trace of the polarisation tendencies that have inflicted other labour markets during the same period. As is well known, the Swedish model is based on powerful labour unions with a strongly egalitarian strategy (they have explicitly tried to block the expansion of low-value-added activities), as well as a highly redistributive welfare state model. Perhaps less widely recognised though is the fundamental acceptance by Swedish trade unions of the need to innovate and modernise the economic system, even if that means layoffs and restructuring. In fact, Swedish unions have traditionally played a significant role in restructuring processes from the very beginning, engaging in local polities to reskill and reallocate the displaced workers. These key elements of the Nordic model could be a crucial part of a modern labour market agenda in the EU.[4]

CHALLENGE TWO: BALANCE THE EMU SHORTCOMINGS WITH COORDINATED AND REDISTRIBUTIVE POLICIES

In terms of social and employment outcomes, the 2008 crisis has been a harsh awakening from the European dream of previous years. In the first decade of the euro, it seemed as if economic integration could on its own act as a force of socioeconomic convergence between the rich and the poor European countries, fulfilling the implicit promises of the European project. Yet the crisis recast that period as a mirage, the result of unsustainable developments that would cruelly reverse after 2008, wiping off a significant part of the progress previously achieved.[5] This has led to the recognition that, after all, economic and monetary integration on its own – without significant coordination of social and employment policies, nor EU-level redistribution mechanisms – is a force which creates divergence, not convergence. Even worse, it can result in a 'race-to-the-bottom' process of downward convergence, in which social standards are used as factors of adjustment in the absence of other mechanisms.

So what can be done? A progressive labour market agenda within any European country must recognise the need to step up EU coordination of social and employment policies and develop EU-level redistribution mechanisms.[6] In the context of European economic integration, a narrow national labour market agenda is bound to fail in many important respects. An example of such EU-level mechanisms is the idea of European coordination of minimum wage policies.[7] Aiming at a commonly agreed minimum relative level (the most frequently mentioned is 60 per cent of the median national wage, although there are many possible alternatives) could be a powerful tool for preventing vicious processes of racing to the bottom. Such a move would strengthen demand while minimising negative effects on the competitiveness of countries with respect to other European economies.

The difficulties for such coordination would be mostly institutional, due to the wide diversity in existing systems of minimum wage setting across Europe (with some countries having statutory universal wage floors and others collectively agreed sector-specific minima). The countries with strong collective bargaining traditions have historically feared that EU-level coordination on these issues could erode the autonomy of social partners. However, options that allow for an effective harmonisation of minimum wage levels while respecting the existing diversity in the systems of minimum wage setting could and should be explored. Another example of this type of EU-level coordination and integration that is being discussed is a European unemployment scheme to complement existing national systems.[8] Such a scheme would protect national labour markets against asymmetric shocks such as the one suffered after 2008, acting not only as an economic stabiliser, but also as a powerful counterbalance to the centrifugal effects of European economic integration.

CHALLENGE THREE: THE COMING OF ROBOTS AND THE FUTURE OF EUROPEAN EMPLOYMENT

The final challenge I would like to discuss is much more far-fetched and less certain than the previous two. Still, its potential implications are so vast that in my view any modern labour market agenda has to take it into account. In recent decades, human civilisation has massively expanded its capacity to process, store and communicate information. This development, which is proceeding at an accelerating pace, is precipitating a generalised increase in the rate of innovation in many different fields, with subsequent rounds of cross-fertilisation and synergies between them that suggest further acceleration in the future. For example, separate developments in the fields of robotics, artificial intelligence and cloud computing are converging in 'cloud robotics', an innovation which allows cheap connected robots to learn from the experiences of each other and expand their overall competence massively.

These technological developments have obvious wide-ranging implications for all aspects of human civilisation. But probably the most important implications are those for the economy, understood in a broad sense. The possibility of creating highly autonomous robots that could do most of the tasks currently done by human workers seems reachable in the not-so-distant-future. This conjures visions of Arcadia, a final emancipation from work and the toils imposed by the material conditions of our existence. Yet the coming of an age of robots conjures dystopian images also. A fundamental pillar of our current socioeconomic system is that the distribution of the fruits of production is linked to participation in such production, which for the vast majority of the population takes the form of labour input. Under these parameters, a production process totally carried out by robots would exclude most of the population from any access to the material wealth created: the owners of the robots would receive all the income. Of course, such a system would be unsustainable in its own terms, since there would be hardly any demand for the goods and services produced by the robots. But what this scenario shows is that the technological developments we are entertaining may require a radical rethinking of the main principles of our political economy, particularly the link between the spheres of production and distribution.

Many argue that fears of large-scale technological unemployment are fundamentally wrong. After all, technology has been displacing labour since the agricultural revolution, and society has always found ways to allocate the excess labour, mainly through the emergence of new activities and services made possible by the increased levels of productivity and surplus. But previous large-scale technological revolutions have led to massive disruptions to the social fabric, and declines in living standards that could last generations (as testified by the social conditions of the English working class during the industrial revolution). Further to this, it is possible that this time is different: a level of technology in which machines can do all or most types of unpleasant tasks could certainly create a very different type of society, where the concept of work would have a very different meaning.

What can be done? This is such a long-term challenge that it is difficult to say anything practical or sensible on what to do about it. And yet it seems reasonable to argue that we should start thinking about how to reorganise our socioeconomic systems in order to deal with the potential implications of a generalised substitution of human labour by robots. As previously mentioned, the key challenge is how to deal with the fact that on its own, such a development could exclude the general population from the fruits of progress. The economist Richard Freeman, echoing previous proposals of 'people's capitalism', suggests a policy of expanding the ownership of robots/capital to workers, who would then benefit from the income they generate.[9] A radically different strategy would be to explicitly decouple the distribution of income from participation in production, by using some form of universal guaranteed income scheme financed by taxes. These ideas may seem far-fetched, but it seems likely that labour market agendas will incorporate them in a not so distant future.

NOTES

1. Eurofound (2015) *Upgrading or polarisation? Long-term and Global Shifts in the Employment Structure*, Publications Office of the European Union, Luxembourg.

2. Eurofound (2014) *Pay in Europe in the 21st Century*, Publications Office of the European Union, Luxembourg.

3. Fernandez-Macias, E., Hurley, J. & Storrie, D. (2012) *Transformation of the Employment Structure in the EU and USA, 1995–2007*, Basingstoke: Palgrave Macmillan; Fernandez-Macias, E. (2012) 'Job Polarization in Europe? Changes in the Employment Structure and Job Quality, 1995–2007', *Work and Occupations*, 39(2), pp. 157–82.

4. This approach is in fact similar to the concept of flexicurity which was not so long ago promoted by European institutions, although it quickly became discredited because they made too much emphasis on the flexibility and too little on the security side. It should be obvious that for such an approach to work, both aspects have to be equally emphasized.

5. Eurofound (2015) *Recent Developments in the Distribution of Wages in Europe*, Publications Office of the European Union, Luxembourg.

6. Alternatively, it could defend a rollback of European economic and monetary integration (including the Euro): but that would probably precipitate a massive economic crisis and possibly a collapse of the whole European project, with all its frightening implications. And in any case, that is an entirely different discussion.

7. Fernández-Macías, E. & Vacas-Soriano, C. (2015) 'A Coordinated European Union Minimum Wage Policy?', *European Journal of Industrial Relations* (Published online before print, 16 October 2015).

8. Dullien, S. (2014) *A European Unemployment Benefit Scheme. How to Provide for More Stability in the Euro Zone*, Gütersloh: Bertelsmann-Stiftung, 5.

9. Freeman, R. B. (2015) *Who Owns the Robots Rules the World*. IZA World of Labor.

Part IV

Politics: Coalition-Building in an Age of Political Fragmentation

THE FUTURE IS AN OPPORTUNITY, NOT A THREAT – IF PROGRESSIVES GET THE MESSAGE RIGHT

Frank Stauss

People around the world are anxious about the future, and it does not matter whether their economy is in a current recession or performing quite well. Even the Germans – where in 2015 about 75 per cent of people according to recent polls consider their personal financial situation as 'good' or 'very good' – are anxious about the future. In their rather pessimistic disposition, they obviously do not see themselves as a nation that got out of the European crisis sooner than any other. The Germans see themselves as the ones closer than any other to the next crisis. Remember, currently about 2.9 million Germans are unemployed (6.9 per cent). During the climax of the crisis in 2005, the number totalled 4.8 million (12 per cent). Bringing unemployment down by 2 million took enormous efforts, tough cuts in the social system and a decade's worth of work. Not exactly a quick fix.

But the state of the German mind might give us a head start of what to expect in other nations after an extremely long and deep period of crisis: confidence in the future will not be the same.

Anxiety about the future actually seems to be an overall state of mind no matter how good or bad the present is. In Germany this is confirmed by virtually all our focus groups, no matter the region in which people live, how old they are or whether they belong to the upper, middle, or working class. No one feels safe.

And why should they? They sense that the way we live, work, travel, communicate and participate is currently in the middle of a transition, if not a revolution. They may not be able to give us a detailed analysis of what the future holds for them but even well-paid workers at a Mercedes-Benz plant openly discuss whether their products will stand the test of the next two decades. This would have previously been an unthinkable thought in 1960, 1990 or even 2010.

The distance from anxiety to hope is a long way. The distance from anxiety to fear is markedly shorter.

But progressives can never be defenders of the past or preservers of the status quo. It is not how we operate. Standing still and defending old habits is the specialty of conservatives; they will always be better at that, and we will always feel bad trying.

Most of all, progressives will never be the party of fear. It is the territory of rightwing or leftwing populism and hate. Fear will never be a formula for success for progressives.

A time of progress must be a time for progressives. Change is inevitable – and who should be better prepared for change than us?

The time we live in is a chance of massive proportion for progressives to dominate the political, economic and social debate for decades. Are we ready to see and seize this chance? And are we willing and prepared to learn from past mistakes to frame the future debate according to our core values?

Framing a debate the 'progressive way' demands confidence in our beliefs, and our beliefs are almost never the beliefs of our opponents. We must not adopt conservatism and conservative solutions; we must frame the debate our way.

We embrace and are willing to design and define a future with more equality, more prosperity, more transparency, better health, better education, and more chances. We are the ones who always stood and fought for a modern economy, a modern society, modern families and a future that will always be better than the past or the present. So who should be better in shaping a good future but us?

To achieve this we cannot ignore risks and wrong turns. We must not follow every path opening before us; some of these paths will not lead to progress, but to a major backlash. Not everything that is new is also good. What is good has to be approved by our standards. Will it bring mankind ahead or will it just lead to lower wages, self-exploitation, longer working hours and less privacy? If the latter is the case, it is not a path we follow.

It is our job to distinguish between good and bad. We have to lead. Voters are demanding a clear direction, because they will not notice any other.

When people are anxious or even afraid, they start looking for leadership. To provide this leadership, our signals have to be strong and clear.

With the rise of the internet and almost unlimited access to information for almost every person within the EU, campaigners once envisioned a new type of voter: the fully informed citizen, caring about society as well for their personal wellbeing, of the nation, the European Union and the world, getting up on election day, entering the polling station, and making a rational decision. What we observe is quite the opposite. The multichannel information opportunities are opportunities for disinformation, non-information and confusion.

We observe a massive information tune-out, with more and more people leaving the ground we once considered common knowledge. The gap between the highly informed elites and the vast majority of the people is widening – not closing. While more and more people are channelling the information they are willing to receive, knowledge about politics, economics and culture is losing the battle versus entertainment, sports and special interests.

In times of a daily paper and only several TV and radio stations, a media consumer still achieved what I call 'collateral knowledge'. Once you opened the paper with the sports section, you later moved on to local news, politics, economics and maybe even the feuilleton, simply because you paid for it and wanted your money's worth of the paper; that is history.

In our recent campaigns, with limited resources (data access, money, people) compared to some massive US campaigns, we turned away from micro-targeting to 'the big idea', or, as George Bush Sr once called it: "the vision thing". We did however send a strong emotional message: a message of hope v fear. A message, that the future will be better, not worse – if we take the right direction now.

When in 1875 the founders of the SPD came together in the city of Gotha, their aim was to make the lives of millions of workers and their families better. They cared not only for better conditions at the workplace but also for better education, better housing, better medical treatment and more. They founded their movement at a time when there was neither a democracy nor much hope to gain as much influence as needed to make their programme come true. At the heart of this movement was hope. Hope that things could be turned to the better, no matter how strong the opponents or how unlikely the chance for success.

Today almost no one in Germany has to be afraid of hunger and even the poorest are provided with good housing conditions. Education is accessible to everybody and, even if there are remaining issues of inequality by heritage, it is possible for every child to climb up the ladder with the help of free kindergarten to free preschool, free college and free universities.

Some even consider 'the work done', with the social democrats being victims of their own success. That could not be further from the truth. This is because in a dramatically changing world, almost nothing is more out of sync with what needs to be done but conservatism.

A world in motion is a world for progressives.

So what are the challenges of our times, besides the obvious like mass migration or ongoing wars in many regions of the world – even in Europe?

The challenges of our times are mostly all connected to the digital revolution. The digital revolution will change the way we live much more fundamentally than any of the previous revolutions. What has been labelled 'Industry 4.0' and 'Work 4.0' will inevitably lead to 'Life 4.0', and people are beginning to notice.

They are beginning to notice that we are not just talking about the comfort of a mobile phone, easy access to information and permanent working hours in a global economy. They are beginning to notice that every aspect of their life will somehow be changed with or through the digital revolution and global connectivity.

People experience the falling behind of regions without state of the art access to the digital world. They see mass migration to Europe based on information provided thorough the web and migrants staying in touch with their loved ones or getting the latest border information through their ever present smart phone.

Highly trained employees witness the falling behind of their premium companies when it comes to connectivity and digital progress. The cashier in the supermarket wonders about whether they will be needed five years from now – not 50. If companies like Nokia rise to global dominance and almost disappear within a decade, what is to say that will not nations rise and fall faster than ever before in history?

There are clearly so many questions, yet there are so few answers. Questions about how we work, questions of privacy v transparency, of family lives, of community, property, the distribution of wealth and knowledge, in some nations of diversity, demographic change and the necessity of migration.

One path into a better future certainly is the wrong one; the path backward.

Trying to find solutions for the future in the past never worked.

It is the job of progressives to define the future and to finally frame a debate ahead of the challenges. We can no longer abuse ourselves as the repair-unit of Europe.

But to be ahead of the challenges, we have to stay awake, be alert, stay curious and we have to permanently question our programmes. Are we still ahead of our time? Are we providing answers to current questions, or have we hidden ourselves behind solutions for a world of yesterday? If we want to beat conservatives and accuse them of being too slow for change, too negative about the future, too much defenders of the past, then are we ready to be the opposite?

Are we ready for the biggest battle: hope v fear?

To frame the debate, progressives have to make one thing very clear: what we have achieved so far is not threatened by change, but by ignorance. Ignoring the changes around us takes away the ability to design the future. Neglect means taking the elevator down, not up. People do understand that very well. They are not stupid, but so far nobody is talking to them like they are adults. Most parties treat them like children who need to be protected from the crazy world outside of the *kinderzimmer*.

Let us begin by taking the voters seriously and by starting a debate on what they already know; ignorance is not the answer. A narrative for progressives in a changing world. Change is inevitable.

Whether it is a change for the better or for the worse is ours to decide. We believe that the best is yet to come.

And we have proven in the past that the change progressives stood and stand for always was and is a change for the better. Most of all, we were always ahead of our time and not behind.

We have always looked to fight for better education for all children, while conservatives cared more about status, hierarch and inequality. We have always fought for better working conditions, greater distribution of wealth, the furthering of workers' rights and stronger participation. We have always fought for more transparency, stronger democracy, greater equality and a cleaner environment long before anyone else did. And we have fought for women's rights, equal pay regardless of whether you are a man or a woman, the rights of minorities, and a more diverse society as the direct source of a stronger sense of community, and a better use of talent.

With all of these fights, causes and progressions, we can say one thing for certain; history is on our side.

We were right, and they were wrong. But the world keeps on turning – and once again it is within our grasps and abilities to design the future.

We must fight for a modern society where no child is abandoned by the state, no matter the circumstances that that child grows up in, whether it be the 'the classic family', a patchwork family, raised by a single-parent, by homosexual parents or by heterosexual parents.

We must fight for societies with a fair balance concerning the distribution of wealth, because fair societies have proven to be more stable, stronger economically and to have a better sense of community. They also have proven to be stronger at innovating, and stronger in providing a better quality of life, something which is fundamental to society.

We must fight for a new digital society where 24/7 digitalisation goes hand in hand with the right to free time, privacy, improved working conditions, and where success is measured in living qualities. The future working place must be better than the ones of the past – and we must take care of that.

We must fight for a modern industry with more success through innovation and ecologically sound technology. Old industries fail in the long run, and state of the art production prevails.

We must fight for affordable healthcare, social security, affordable housing in ever-increasingly expensive cities, top quality infrastructure (including mass transportation and unlimited access to digital technologies).

With all of these causes that we must endeavour with, like the causes which we have championed previously and continue to champion, the future will prove us right.

All of this is crucial for a good society; all of this is crucial for a great society.

The road to success is a blunt and promising vision; 'hope v fear' is the battleground.

We will define the frame of the future if we are willing and able to take risks and to make decisions. We must decide what is good and what is bad according to our values and we must be ready to endure and fight the battles following our decisions.

Progressive parties – or some of them – behaved like cowards rather than leaders in the past; they lacked inspiration, defended the status quo, were lazy thinkers, adopted neoliberal laissez faire or socialist overprotection, and reduced themselves to micromanagement and daily business.

But who will follow a coward? Who desires for a living compromise? Who is willing to elect a repairman? Who is thrilled by an excel chart? Who will get overly enthusiastic about a natural number two?

No matter which position a progressive party is in right now, whether it be in government, in opposition, or in a governing coalition as the smaller partner, the next campaign has to be about the future and clear about the alternatives we espouse.

Conservatives in some countries adopted rhetoric of change while actually delivering gridlock, old recipes, nationalism or regionalism and fantasies of a world that could be designed as if it were a century ago.

Change, as mentioned above, can bring out the best and the worst in politics. To fight the worst, we have to bring out the best in ourselves. Which is a positive look at the future?

The next campaign should not worry about target groups etc in the first place but about the main message: an invitation to all voters and even other parties to join our movement for change. Whoever wants to work on a positive future is our guest, our partner, our possible fellow and coalition companion.

I am sure that the majority of people would rather follow our path of hope instead of the path of fear. Uncertain times are times for leaders and clear leadership. We can take that lead.

To be blunt, we have to take over that lead. Progressive leadership is our heritage and our future.

IF POLITICAL PARTIES WERE STARTUPS ...

Guillaume Liegey

"**W**e are all broken, every single one of us, and yet we pretend that we are not". This is how one of the greatest Democratic party candidates once described the state of progressive politics in America in a convention speech.

Matt Santos – the Democratic party nominee in the sixth series of the political TV drama *The West Wing* – gave his speech over a decade ago. Yet the statement sounds just as relevant today to describe how most European progressive parties are perceived, both by insiders and outside observers. Something is wrong with progressive parties in Europe. Like many established organisations, progressive parties have been challenged by the decline of their traditional 'clientele' and the rise of alternative players. For cab drivers, it is Uber and company. For political parties, these are Avaaz, Change. org, Podemos or the Five Star Movement. These organisations have created new civic engagement models that look more appealing to citizens of the 21st century. In doing so, they have fuelled the debate on the relevance and the survival of traditional political parties.

Let's make it clear: I am convinced that political parties will survive. The question is how they can be better at capturing the tremendous demand for civic engagement. My answer is simple: they have to become indispensable organisations that provide indispensable services to their people.

I am the founder of a campaign strategy startup and for the past five years I have been following closely – and sometimes helping to implement – innovations in political campaigning. However the ideas that this paper goes on to discuss do not draw so much from my experience as a campaigner but rather as the founder of a startup.

What do I mean by startup? It is a company that has not yet found a successful business model but is in the process of addressing the right questions to eventually do so. And these questions are straightforward. Which problems do I solve, and are these problems important? Who are the people I serve, and how do I solve their problems? How are my solutions better than those of existing players?

All successful startups have found their answers to these questions and have become indispensable to their customers. Yet this does not seem to be the case for most political parties today. When political parties find their way to answer these questions – when they manage to define their missions and offer tools to fulfil them – they will gradually become indispensable organisations in the realm of progressive civic engagement.

In this paper, I suggest four issues for the party of the future to solve. I believe these issues are important and that progressive political parties are the best suited to tackle them. The mission of the party of the future should entail the following objectives, making such a party indispensable to society:

- To become the Greenpeace for social justice: effectively promoting a progressive agenda, starting redistribution and tackling inequality
- To launch a war machine to increase voter turnout in the long run
- To become an incubator for people who want to have an impact on society in line with progressive values
- To harvest all of the left's talents to lead the government of the future

I believe each of these objectives is achievable and I am suggesting a first realistic, testable roadmap to reach them.

BECOMING THE GREENPEACE FOR SOCIAL JUSTICE: EFFECTIVELY PROMOTING A PROGRESSIVE AGENDA, STARTING WITH REDISTRIBUTION AND TACKLING INEQUALITY

In 2014, the French economist Thomas Piketty became the champion of redistribution when he published his book *Capital in the 21st* Century. He helped kick off a fierce debate on inequality and redistributive policies. The sudden fame of Piketty and his book's impact came as a pleasant surprise for many progressives, who rejoiced in watching Piketty advocate for redistribution, in newsrooms, universities and banker's conference rooms around the world.

Does it mean that the Piketty world tour was sufficient to ensure that inequality and redistribution are at the centre of public policy discussions? Among a few of Barack Obama's economic advisers maybe. But when it comes to public opinion, the picture looks very different. Inequality is rarely the number one priority for a simple reason: most people underestimate it. This is true no matter how rich or poor they are or how equal or unequal their country is. Misperceiving Inequality, a fascinating study by economists Vladimir Gimpelson and Daniel Treisman compared people's perception of inequality in their country with the actual degree of inequality.[1] The results are stunning: everyone underestimates inequality. And it does not go without consequences for public policy: when people perceive inequality as a moderate problem, they are much more unlikely to accept redistributive policies.

We have more work to do to reach a consensus on the urgency of solving inequality, and this is a mission for the party of the future. Almost all progressive politicians – from the heirs of Blairism to the French *frondeurs* (rebels) via Matteo Renzi's supporters – would agree that inequality is one of the key issues in progressive politics. Yet, no European social democratic party could be called the Greenpeace of inequality. Why is Thomas Piketty much more vocal and effective at doing the work of progressive parties? I cannot see any reason why progressive parties should not be better at pushing for a more redistributive agenda.

And it is possible to shape the political agenda. Conservatives have often proved it, from George W Bush's campaign against the inheritance tax (relabelled 'death tax'), to the UK Independence party and French Front National's anti-EU and anti-immigration diatribes. In 2013, the Manif pour Tous (Demo for All) – opponents to gay marriage in France – built a powerful movement that reached beyond traditional conservative activists. They managed to hack the legislative process by slowing the debates in parliament and gained national exposure to defend their arguments.

As Gaël Brustier and David Djaïz have argued in an essay for the Paris-based Jean-Jaurès Foundation,[2] I believe the party of the future can also win the battle of ideas and become an effective advocate of a progressive agenda, especially on redistribution. But this requires 'getting out of the building', a commandment for startuppers to remind them they will never find nor understand their customers while sitting in an office. They have to proactively engage with them. This holds true for political parties, whose members too rarely get out of the building.

GET OUT OF THE BUILDING TO UNDERSTAND HOW PEOPLE LIVE AND PERCEIVE INEQUALITY

Working on public opinion's perception of inequality is necessary to create more acceptability for redistributive policies. Organising an effective advocacy campaign hence starts with understanding people's perception. How? Well, opinion polls, studies and focus groups are of course one way to go. But they are not enough. What do startups do to understand their public's needs? They get out of the building and talk first-hand and spend time – a lot of time – with their customers, so that they end up thinking and feeling like they are one on them. Everybody in the company has to engage with customers at some point, not just salespeople.

For political parties, getting out of the building means sending as many party activists as possible to engage directly with citizens at their doorsteps to conduct a qualitative field survey. This survey can be targeted at specific demographic groups or at neighbourhoods with a high electoral potential. Gather a group of 20 activists and after a week of door knocking, they will have had a five- to seven-minute conversation with 1,000 people; ask them to let themselves become immersed in people's lives, to remember individual stories and quotes on how what inequality means to people. It is worth emphasising that at this stage the intent is to collect information, not to start advocating for more redistributive policies.

Draft Arguments That Stick

Once you have a better understanding of what people think, you can start drafting the arguments for your campaign. The science of effective arguments is complex. What parties often do is assemble a sales pitch with a list of supposedly striking figures. They use them to bombard their opponents in televised debates, with little lasting effect on the audience. A successful advocacy campaign makes its arguments stick with the audience. How? Arguments that stick combine simplicity, unexpectedness, concreteness, credibility, emotions and stories, according to the bible of sticky arguments, the book *Made to Stick*, by Chip and Dan Heath.[3] The way that the authors reshuffle the argument to convince that America spends too little on foreign aid is enlightening.[4] *Made to Stick* should become the bedside reading of any politicians of the future.

Communicate Effectively

The ultimate question is the channel of communication. How to reach people you want to convince? The key is to ensure the party reaches far beyond its core members and supporters, who are highly likely to share the same beliefs and do not need to be convinced. Successful advocacy campaigns combine targeted and non-targeted communications, from door-to-door sessions organised by party activists to politicians sharing their sticky arguments on TV and through all imaginable progressive platforms. There are many examples of such campaigns; look, for example, at the British member of parliament Stella Creasy's campaign on payday loans.[5] Imagine how powerful a campaign would be if it combined politicians on TV, powerful op-eds in national and local newspapers and thousands of party activists knocking at doors, all bombarding public opinion with sticky arguments on inequality.

Which goal should such a campaign set? Successful startups demonstrate three-figure growth rate. Let's start with a humble and realistic objective: to increase by 10 percentage points within two years the share of citizens who answer "yes" to the question "Should government's policies be more redistributive?"

RUNNING A WAR MACHINE TO INCREASE TURNOUT IN THE LONG RUN

All democracies face a decline in turnout, which affects all ballots, from low salience local elections to presidential races. Non-voters represent such a large share of the electorate that get-out-the-vote operations are now part of every campaigner's toolkit. Today, we do know one tactic that usually works to increase turnout for elections: knocking at doors.

The first evidence of the power of direct interaction came from the seminar work of Alan Gerber and Donald Green.[6] Their randomised control trial in New Haven in 1998 opened the way for the comeback of door-to-door canvassing in US campaigns and later on in many European countries. But, as great as the impact of door-to-door can be to mobilise voters for an election, it can only be a short-term solution. Too often, canvassers disappear right after election day and rarely come back before the next cycle. This is obviously insufficient to tackle the long-run decline of turnout.

What is required is to create sustainable political engagement among citizens who stopped voting or never have voted, and who doubt the ability of politics to effectively solve their problems. An increasing number of citizens feel that politics is a foreign and distant world and politicians are unable to understand their concerns and expectations. If you feel politics is powerless and ignores you, why indeed bother voting?

The party of the future should find a more sustainable solution to foster political engagement. How? Force its members to get out of the building!

Get Out of the Building (Again)

The party of the future would make it a rule that its members spend 70 per cent of their activist time engaging with people outside of the party. In France, several local units of the Socialist party have established weekly door-to-door sessions outside of campaign periods. Members promote the activities of their unit, provide information on government reforms and occasionally (though this is never a priority) recruit new members. A nationally coordinated advocacy campaign on inequality could easily provide a great alibi to get out of the building. The same rule should apply to elected officials, from local councillors to members of parliament, and become a routine in their weekly schedule.

Other formats could be experimented with, like small town hall meetings where a politician would have the opportunity to engage in a conversation with no more than 10 citizens. The governing principle for the conversation should be kept simple and strict: citizens talk 80 per cent of the time, the politician 20 per cent. The key success factor of this format is the selection of the group of citizens: they cannot be party members or supporters but are chosen because they do not easily have access to politicians. Conversely, many politicians lose touch with citizens once elected, not because they enjoy the ivory-tower atmosphere but because political offices schedules are very demanding and do not make field work a basic requirement. The party of the future can help by organising these small-group conversations.

Another idea would be to send politicians to schools in low-turnout areas and have them explain why they engaged in politics and why it matters to them. It should not necessarily replace more formal civic education classes but provide a more personal perspective on why political engagement, starting with voting, matters. "To be ashamed of miseries you did not cause" – this is how Donald Berwick, a candidate for the Democratic primary for Massachusetts' gubernatorial election in 2010, described what drove him to public service and political engagement. A line like this one might stick better in one's mind than the explanation of the rationale behind the separation of powers.

The party of the future could launch experiments with these ideas and scale up those that work, primarily in the lowest-turnout neighbourhoods. And it should again set a humble and realistic goal – how about increasing turnout by five percentage points over two years in neighbourhoods with the lowest turnout?

BECOMING AN INCUBATOR FOR PEOPLE WHO WANT TO HAVE AN IMPACT ON SOCIETY IN LINE WITH PROGRESSIVE VALUES

Many community organisations promote political engagement and offer an alternative approach to traditional politics (see for example the Leading Change Network, the Movement for Change or the 'transition movement'[7]). This does not mean that political parties should see them as competitors on the civic engagement market. Potential synergies between political parties and community organisations are immense.

What could the party of the future do for organisers and activists? What do they need to promote their cause? Training, checklists, toolkits, funds (a little), encouragement (a lot) and sometimes a little push for publicity. Political parties have expertise on most of these dimensions and a unique asset to offer: scale. In a nutshell, the party of the future can act as an incubator and help community organisations reach a scale very few of them are likely to reach on their own. It can help connect community organisations to party members and supporters willing to start a fight together. It can help raise funds since they have access to a precious database of politically engaged citizens. It can help generate publicity for selected community organising projects and promote them at the national level, something a local community organiser would struggle to achieve alone.

Conversely, the party of the future could work with them to reach out to citizens who feel abandoned by politics and partner with organisations that aim – for example – at increasing turnout, like Rock the Vote in the US. Also, it remains quite a challenge to make community organising accessible to a wider group of citizens. Educated and politically engaged citizens are usually more susceptible to organise to defend their ideas and they are very likely to have access to policymakers. The party of the future should ensure that less politically connected citizens also benefit from community organising expertise and offer joint training programs with community organisations, with a specific effort to reach out to citizens in neighbourhoods where political and civic engagement is limited.

Becoming an inclusive incubator for community organising projects is a great way for parties to become indispensable to organisations they collaborate with and to their own members. I am convinced many of them would be keen to find opportunities to engage in civic projects beyond the traditional party activities. For example, in France several NGOs work to support asylum seekers while their application is reviewed.[8] In many cases, they do not have any housing options and the state does not provide any solutions during the application review. NGOs recruit families who are willing to host one asylum seeker for a short stay, usually five weeks. Why could the French Socialist party not offer to connect these NGOs with their members who are willing to help?

When the party of the future becomes a successful incubator, not only will it be seen as more indispensable but it will also send a great signal to those who think politics is disconnected from reality since it will have many examples of actual – and positive – impact on people's lives.

HARVESTING ALL THE LEFT'S TALENTS TO LEAD THE GOVERNMENT OF THE FUTURE

One of political parties' core missions in a democracy is the supply of political leaders. There is a clear discontent with political leaders today, which suggests that selection is part of the problem. Over the years, defiance towards politicians continues to increase: 89 per cent of French citizens think politicians do not care about their expectations, a 40-percentage-point increase since the 1980s. In the UK, citizens say they trust politicians less than bankers.[9] Similar statements could be made across Europe.

One explanation is that political parties struggle to attract talents and diversify the profile of their candidates. Leading the government of the future will require new skillsets and experience that extends beyond navigating the maze of internal party politics. But there is still a glass wall between career politics and other careers. How can the party of the future bring more diversity among their own candidates? It should do what startups do when they look for talents: they go headhunting. It should proactively search for people with an interesting background, approach them, and offer to coach them before they stand for office.

Though the perfect candidate cannot be manufactured from scratch, the party of the future could do a lot to pick out promising talents and coach them to become great candidates and, if elected, great political leaders. To design an effective curriculum, it can look at successful examples in the United States, with the Wellstone Institute and the New Organizing Institute. Both offer high-quality training, building on a long experience of running campaigns and working with progressive politicians. The party of the future could first set up a partnership with these organisations and send a small group of 10–15 candidates to take part in training sessions in the US, before developing their own programmes internally.

It should also set a clear, measurable objective and for example save 25 per cent of their seats for these profiles, not only in constituencies where they are unlikely to win. And this could be done at any level: municipal, regional, national. To limit the resistance against what could be perceived as 'parachuting', these candidates should be chosen locally whenever possible and, if not, local party organisations should be involved in the selection process. The coaching curriculum should include field activities with local party activists.

The party of the future can also help politicians already in office become more innovative and organise regular international study tours, a very powerful way to discover innovations and get energised about them. These study tours are not the same as traditional ministers' visits. They are designed to be working trips, with very specific interview guides to collect information. Two years ago, it is during such a study tour that I discovered Enroll America. This non-profit organisation, led by Anne Filipic, was set up to assist the implementation of the Affordable Care Act. Enroll America has been using many lessons from the Obama campaigns, from predictive modelling to target eligible people to campaign techniques, from neighbourhood meetings to door-to-door canvassing. They have worked to inform eligible people about Obamacare and explain how they can benefit from the reform; enrolment campaigns organised by Enroll America have helped insure more than 11 million citizens. If politicians and policymakers in France and Europe were more aware of such initiatives – if they could feel the passion of those who started them – they would be energised and more likely to experiment with similar projects at home. I am not certain that everything would work but it would help spur a more open state of mind – one more prone to experiment.

To current and prospective party leaders, I would conclude by saying that these ideas can all be implemented in a reasonable amount of time. They are workable within the existing party infrastructure and can provide a powerful source for inspiration for existing and future members. Another great fake politician, President Jed Bartlett, once said: "Never doubt that a small group of thoughtful committed citizens can change the world". Let's make sure the party of the future is the choice of preference for such people.

NOTES

1. Gimpelson, V. & Treisman, D. (2015) 'Misperceiving inequality', *National Bureau of Economic Research*, Working Paper 21174, http://www.nber.org/papers/w21174.pdf.

2. Brustier, G. & Djaïz, D. (2013) 'The tools of cultural struggle: Ten proposals for the Socialist party', *Fondation Jean Jaurès*, http://www.jean-jaures.org/Publications/Notes/Les-outils-du-combat-culturel.-Dix-propositions-pour-le-Parti-socialiste.

3. Heath, C. & Heath, D. (2007) *Made to Stick: Why Some Ideas Survive and Others Die*, New York: Random House.

4. Heath, C. & Heath, D. (2007) 'Does America Spend Too Much on Foreign Aid?', in: *Made to Stick: Why Some Ideas Survive and Others Die*, New York: Random House.

5. Creasy, S. (2013) 'The case for capping payday loan rates is overwhelming', *The Guardian*, http://www.theguardian.com/commentisfree/2013/mar/06/payday-loan-rates-capping.

6. Gerber, A. S. & Green, D. P. (1999) 'Does canvassing increase voter turnout? A field experiment', *Proceedings of the National Academy of Sciences of the United States of America*, 96(19), pp. 10939–42, http://www.pnas.org/content/96/19/10939.full?ck=nck.

7. Euractiv (2014) 'UN official: EU needs to encourage social movements', *Euractiv*, http://www.euractiv.com/section/sustainable-dev/interview/un-official-eu-needs-to-encourage-social-movements/.

8. Baumard, M. (2015) 'Ghiath, demandeur d'asile syrien accueilli par la famille Pépin', Le Monde, http://www.lemonde.fr/societe/article/2015/07/29/ces-francais-qui-accueillent-un-demandeur-d-asile_4702994_3224.html.

9. Evans, H. & Skinner, G. (2015) 'Politicians trusted less than estate agents, bankers and journalists', *Ipsos MORI*, https://www.ipsos-mori.com/researchpublications/researcharchive/3504/Politicians-trusted-less-than-estate-agents-bankers-and-journalists.aspx.

REFLECTIONS ON THE CENTRE LEFT IN EUROPE AND LATIN AMERICA

Andrés Velasco

For many of the big issues and challenges in progressive politics today, there is a real contrast between how they are seen in northern Europe and what they look like from Latin American countries such as my own. I would like to reflect on some of the successes and failures of the centre left in Chile, and on how social democrats in Europe and Latin America can learn from each other.

Clearly, the context for centre left politics is different on each continent – most obviously in the level of per capita income, although here one should be wary of exaggeration: to take Greece as an example, its per capita income was only 25 per cent above Chile's before the crisis, and today could well be the lower of the two. A more significant contrast is that Europe has been in a fiscal crisis in the past few years, whereas Latin American countries faced their fiscal crises back in the 80s, so fiscal issues are less dominant today. Finally, whereas there tends to be one established social democratic party in most European countries, this is not the case in Latin America, where party systems are more fluid.

Nonetheless, many of the issues faced by social democrats in Europe have parallels in Latin America.

For a start, the Latin American centre left is also under attack from populisms of right and left. In this sense, the political challenge is very much the same. And just as in Europe, in Latin America there is growing distrust of established political parties and established institutions. And again much as in Europe, in Latin America cultural issues are gaining political salience. While immigration is not (yet) a major issue, questions like abortion, marriage equality, and drug policy most definitely are.

In the end, the big challenge for parties of the centre left is the same regardless of country or continent. It is the challenge to reconcile the competing imperatives of equity, fairness, and redistribution on the one hand, and the need for reform, growth and modernisation on the other.

Listening to social democrats across Europe, the impression I get is overwhelmingly one of gloom – rather too much gloom in my opinion. For them, politics seems to be dominated by two presumptions: one economic and the other political.

The economic presumption is that the defining economic issue of the day is austerity. The right favours austerity, the left opposes it, and this division colours political discourse. A common corollary is the idea that since the financial crisis has led to popular distrust of the market economy, and so to be on the left means taking a somewhat anti-capitalist stance.

On the political side the presumption is that society is divided between a socially conservative working class and a liberal professional class, and this creates an unsolvable problem for the left, whose traditional working class base is opposed to the liberal values of its more cosmopolitan leadership.

From the perspective of the Latin American centre left, these presumptions could not be more wrong. Some of the successes of progressive politics both in Chile and across our continent make this clear.

For a start, in Chile (as in many other Latin American countries as well as in Scandinavia) we have been able to redefine the terms of debate: fiscal responsibility a progressive cause. One of my proudest days in politics was when I heard my boss, President Bachelet, a woman of the left, a socialist, an exile, and a symbol of resistance against Augusto Pinochet, get up and give a speech in which the crowning line was just that – 'fiscal responsibility is a progressive idea'.

Why? Because when you get fiscal policy wrong, and things blow up, who suffers most? The poor. The people who have suffered most in Greece are not the Greeks who have their money deposited in the City of London, but the poor Greeks whose pensions have been cut or who have lost their jobs entirely.

In Latin America the trauma of painful fiscal crises in the 80s made it possible to argue that the first task of centre-left administrations was to show that we could manage our affairs in an orderly fashion. While adopting a fiscal rule and running surpluses was politically difficult in the short term, it meant that when Lehman Brothers went under, in Chile we were sitting on nearly $30bn of cash with a gross public debt of only three per cent of GDP. This meant that in response to a possible recession we could go on a spending spree that would have made Keynes blush.

We launched one of the most ambitiously counter-cyclical fiscal policies in the world, shifting from a surplus of eight per cent of GDP to a deficit of nearly five per cent in one year. President Bachelet left office in 2009 with an 82 per cent approval rating because we could say to people that we saved the money in order to spend it when they needed it most. We spent that money on transfers to households, on emergency house building programs, and on emergency public works programmes. As a result, while the economy did take a hit, the crisis lasted only six or seven months. In Chile we had only two quarters of negative growth; in contrast, Spain had six years of crisis.

Our example shows that it is possible to redefine the fiscal issue in a way that is progressive and economically sound. Of course, being able to run a counter-cyclical policy in crisis situations requires the pain of having saved and repaid debts earlier. To be Keynesian in the down part of the cycle one also has to be Keynesian in the up part of the cycle, saving during booms in order to be able to dis-save during recessions.

In Latin America we also have been able to argue that globalisation, if handled properly, can be a positive force. Chile has 54 free trade agreements with countries collectively accounting for 82 per cent of world GDP. These agreements have paid off in terms of exports, jobs and economic dynamism. Obviously the politics of globalisation is easier in middle income nations than rich nations, since there is no point in protectionism if you do not have a large industrial base to protect. But still it is remarkable that today if you took a random taxi cab in any major city in Latin America and asked the driver 'are free trade agreements good for you?' the chances are that taxi driver would probably say yes – a very different answer to what might be expected in most places in Europe.

Finally, in Latin America at times we have managed to construct a core political constituency around progressive policies that do not cost money. For us the first such measure was achieving the return to human dignity associated with recovering democracy: people understood it to be an achievement and it gave the centre left a good deal of political capital. More recently, strong anti-monopoly / pro-competition policies, strong consumer protection and anti-discrimination policies in the labour market have played a similar political role. They appeal to the concepts of openness and fairness that are key to any modern left-of-centre approach.

In these three broad ways, the Latin American centre left has been able to craft an alternative approach that avoids the gloom and doom that one observes in Europe.

It would be unfair, however, to overlook the areas in which we have failed.

First, in the same way the left in English speaking countries underestimated the need to regulate the financial sector, in Chile and Latin America we underestimated the need to hold the businesses that run many of our public services accountable for the quality of those services. In Chile and Latin America public services including electricity, water, phones and even roads were privatised. People are not upset by the conceptual public-private difference but they do resent failures in the quality of service they get. If your phone company at the end of the month charges $100 for calls you never made, in Chile you would have real trouble getting those charges off your bill, even after queueing in this office and that. This is a trivial example. There are dozens of more serious ones, which causes people to feel they have been abused by private companies because the regulatory framework is not stringent enough.

The second failure is that we have not pulled off the Danish success of redefining what a progressive labour market policy ought to be. I tried this when I was a minister, going to Denmark in what for Chile was a highly publicised trip. We talked about flexicurity, told people that we needed to protect workers and not jobs, and that we needed to beef up insurance and not necessarily subsidies, but we did not get anywhere. In fact the current government of Michelle Bachelet is doing a rather traditional union-oriented (as supposed to flexicurity-oriented) labour reform. This is a real problem in a country like Chile where the failings of the labour market are particularly harsh on women and the young. The overall unemployment rate is not too bad, but the unemployment rate for women and for young people is two and even three times the national average.

In fact, the very skewed income distribution in countries like Brazil, Chile, and Colombia is in large part accounted for by differences in access to jobs. To give a concrete example: in the rich parts of Santiago there are on average 2.5 jobs per household, while in the poor parts the average is 0.5 – that is to say that you have to put two families together to get one steady income. These statistics make it clear that low-income families will remain poor essentially regardless of wage levels because they only on average have half an income in contrast to two-and-a-half incomes on average for wealthy families. Without a new approach to the labour market, closest to what the Scandinavians have done, quality jobs for women and young people will remain scarce. But the politics of reform and moving toward that new approach are nearly impossible.

Failure number three is what I would call the legitimacy-of-democracy failure. With citizens distrustful of political institutions, politicians are seen as all alike. Any legitimacy that might have accrued to politicians by virtue of being on the centre left has pretty much been wiped out. Add to that a slew of controversies and scandals over campaign finance in Chile, or the Petrobras scandal in Brazil, and in the eyes of the public their worst fears about politicians seem to have been confirmed. A poll done in Chile last year asked people which profession they respected most. While the top answer was of course football player, at the very bottom were business leaders, judges, Catholic priests, and last of all members of parliament with only four percent approval. This is not good for the future of democracy in the region.

So to conclude, from a Latin American perspective there are some reasons for optimism, some things to feel proud of, but also a few politically difficult areas in which there has been more failure than success. We still find inspiration in the kinds of ideas that were first put together in Europe. We still see Tony Blair and Gerhard Schröder as examples to follow. Yes Schröder wore very expensive suits and smoked cigars; yes Tony Blair started the wrong war at the wrong time. But their ideas are still worth pursuing. And, as Matteo Renzi has successfully shown, you can do so and be politically successful, getting 40 per cent of the vote or more.

POLITICS IN THE NEW HARD TIMES

Andrew Gamble

Against expectations including their own and the consensus of the polls, the Conservatives won the 2015 election with an overall majority of 12 seats. They had a seven per cent lead over Labour (37 to 30) and 2 million more votes (11 million to 9 million). A relatively small number of seats changed hands. The big losers were the Liberal Democrats who lost 49 of their 57 seats and Labour who lost a net 26 seats. The big winners were the Conservatives who won a net 24 seats and the Scottish National party who won an astonishing 50 seats, taking their tally to 56 out of the 59 Scottish seats. Despite it being such a close election, turnout only rose one per cent to 66 per cent, which meant that the biggest 'party' was once again the non-voters with 34 per cent of the electorate. By contrast the Conservatives won 25 per cent of the electorate and Labour 20 per cent.

The two main parties between them had less than 50 per cent support of the electorate. Labour's vote actually increased by 1.5 per cent and it did win a number of seats, but its gains were overshadowed by its huge strategic reverse in Scotland where it lost 40 out of 41 seats to the SNP, and it failed to win most of its target seats in England. On almost any measure this was a very bad defeat for Labour. It failed to make any progress against the Conservatives and the hurdles it has to surmount to win in 2020 look considerably higher than they were in 2015.

The election victory was a significant one for the Conservatives. Although their share of the vote was still quite low, barely increasing from 2010, their success in winning a majority of seats in parliament was the first time they had done so since 1992. This ended the longest stretch in the modern history of the party without a parliamentary majority. It was also the first time since 1974 that an incumbent government had increased both seats and vote share at a general election, and the first time since 1955 that a government had done so after serving a full parliamentary term. It means that the Conservatives have once again after an absence become the default option in British politics. They have now won six of the nine elections since 1979, the beginning of the neoliberal era. They have confirmed how closely aligned they are with the main structures of interest, property, and media in the UK, and a further strengthening of their position is expected in this parliament with legislation to give effect to English votes for English laws and boundary changes. The Conservative share of the vote may be small. A mandate to govern from only just over one in three of those voting and one in four of the total electorate is weak, but the Conservative position is protected by the first-past-the-post electoral system, and they have no desire or interest to change that.

The reasons Labour lost have been subject to a great deal of analysis already. Powerful accounts include the reports by Patrick Diamond and Giles Radice (*Can Labour Win?*[1]) and by Sally Keeble and Will Straw (*Never Again*[2]). The immediate reasons for the defeat seem plain enough. For the five years of the parliament Labour trailed the Conservatives on who had the best candidate for prime minister and which party the voters trusted to manage the economy. The gap was generally 20 percentage points. Labour's failure to win its argument on the economy and to establish Ed Miliband as an alternative prime minister was symbolised by the final TV debate in the election campaign, when a section of the audience reacted in disbelief to the answers he gave on the origins of the deficit.

But the Conservatives worried that these two advantages, normally so powerful in British electoral politics, were not persuading enough voters to back the Conservatives. Shortly before the election the Conservatives calculated that they were unlikely to win more than 290 seats, not enough to ensure they remained in government. Their response was to develop a third strand to their attack on Labour, warning of the dangers of a minority Labour government kept in office by the votes of the SNP. They questioned the legitimacy of this arrangement as they had questioned the legitimacy of the Liberal government being kept in office by the votes of Irish nationalists after 1910. Whatever the long-term consequences demonising the Scots in this way may have on the future of the union, it had the desired effect on England and was crucial in securing the extra votes the Conservatives needed to ensure they held off Labour's challenge in key marginals and were victorious in so many Liberal Democrat seats. In the election Labour had to fight on three separate fronts: in Scotland, where it was perceived as not sufficiently anti-austerity by voters who deserted it for the SNP; in the north of England, where it was perceived as not sufficiently protectionist by voters who left it for the UK Independence party; and in the south of England and the Midlands, where it was perceived by voters who stayed with the Conservatives as not sufficiently New Labour.

In 2020 Labour will face a big challenge just to maintain the vote it achieved in the 2015 election. What should it do now? Perhaps a little humility is in order for a party that can only command the votes of one in five of the total electorate. In 2018 Labour will have been contesting general elections in a system of universal suffrage for 100 years. In that time there have been 26 general elections. Labour has been in government after only 11 of these. It has been in government with a parliamentary majority after only eight, and with a majority of more than 10 seats after only five. Labour has had 15 leaders before Jeremy Corbyn. Only four of those leaders managed to win an election. Only three of them won a parliamentary majority. Clement Attlee twice, and Harold Wilson and Tony Blair three times. Only Blair won a majority above 10 seats more than once. This is a record which should make the Labour party pause. But apparently not.

THE CORBYN SURGE

After its defeat much of the debate in the Labour party was on whether the priority of the party should be seeking to persuade the voters it had lost to the SNP, to Ukip and to the Conservatives, and whether any strategy could address all three. It also had to assess the way the party had moved under Ed Miliband's leadership. Ed Miliband had argued that the 2008 financial crash and its aftermath had destroyed the consensus on economic policy that had been in place for 30 years and created an opportunity for moving the centre of gravity significantly to the left. At the same time many around him appeared to adopt an electoral strategy that suggested Labour could regain power if it was able to maximise its core vote, estimated to be 35 per cent of the electorate. If it could reach that level then Labour would likely be the single largest party and in a position to form a government either alone or in coalition. Both these strategic choices were shown to be mistaken at the election. Labour failed to convince enough voters that its economic policies were credible, and it failed to achieve 35 per cent of the vote.

In the leadership election which Labour held between June and September 2015 several candidates and commentators argued that the two strategic choices of the Miliband leadership should be abandoned and that the party should adopt a strategy that moved the party back to the political centre, addressing again the concerns of middle England. But the leadership campaign did not go in this direction at all. Instead the party witnessed an insurgency on the left, helped by the new rules adopted in 2012 for leadership elections.

Corbyn was only able to enter the race because 22 members of parliament who did not intend to vote for him were willing to nominate him to ensure that all points of view were heard in the campaign. From the beginning Corbyn was the only candidate who generated energy and excitement, attracting a huge number of young people to join the party as registered supporters, as well as encouraging many who had left the party because of Iraq and other issues to rejoin.

Corbyn fairly quickly established himself as the frontrunner, a position he never seemed in danger of losing. A rank outsider, with odds of 100/1 at the outset ended the campaign with odds of 1/16. He duly won the leadership on the first round of the ballot with the support of almost 60 per cent of the 423,000 votes cast. He had clear majorities in all three categories of voters, and a plurality among registered and affiliated supporters. This has given him a mandate no Labour leader has had since Blair. What Corbyn failed to win (unlike Blair) was the support of Labour MPs. Only 14 are known to have voted for him. His triumph has awakened fears that the party is heading back to a period of sustained internal strife. The relative peace of the Miliband years now looks like a phony peace, and the old divisions in the party and the wider Labour movement now appear to be as strong as they ever were. The risk of another convulsion and bloodletting of the kind which has struck the party every 20 to 30 years of its existence is high.

The surge of support for Corbyn caught everyone by surprise, including Corbyn and most of his backers. Several factors have been involved in his success ranging from the party rule changes which altered the selectorate in ways not predicted. 84 per cent of the new registered supporters voted for Corbyn for example. No one seems to have anticipated the risk of a leader being elected who did not have significant backing among MPs. In the British parliamentary system this has never happened before. Only six per cent of Labour MPs voted for Corbyn, compared to 60 per cent of members. Corbyn's success owes much to the tide of anti-politics and populist protest movements which have become so marked a feature of European politics. What is novel about his victory is that it occurred within an established party rather than arising as an outsider challenge to it.

Corbyn's success reflected the deep dislike many in Labour felt to being on the defensive for so long, and always tacking to the centre. Rediscovering the joys of full-throated opposition, of voting from the heart and on the basis of principles, proved very attractive to many who voted for John Smith in 1992, Tony Blair in 1994, and David and Ed Miliband in 2010. Jeremy Corbyn's platform had little policy detail but its messages of anti-war, anti-austerity, and anti-inequality were very clear and resonated with many existing and returning members and particularly with the thousands of new recruits. Corbyn meetings were packed out and many who attended them spoke of how inspiring he was and of how good it felt to have a candidate who said the things they believed. Corbyn was authentic and unspun, and able to capitalise on the desire to reject the established politics and politicians, as well as providing a powerful new focus for a politics of emotion and identity.

The Corbyn phenomenon also draws on a pervasive sense that old models both of economics and politics have broken down, and old orthodoxies discredited. The new hard times of austerity and deflation, weak economic recovery and rising inequality have fuelled a powerful sense that there must be a better alternative. Many of Corbyn's supporters reject the argument that Ed Miliband's attempted move to the left shows that all moves to the left are bound to fail. They argue rather that Ed Miliband's Labour party was still 'Torylite', still New Labour at its core, unwilling to break decisively from the austerity narrative and set out a radical alternative. This again relates to the authenticity of Corbyn's message. His campaign slogan 'Straight talking, honest politics' captures a great deal of his appeal. In rejecting all the mainstream responses to the crisis Corbyn was able to position himself as the outsider speaking truth to power and offering an escape from the compromises and failures of the past.

Standing back a little from the Corbyn phenomenon its positives and negatives are easy to see. The energy it has brought into politics is an undoubted positive. Just when all established parties appeared to be in long-term decline the Corbyn surge has reversed that. Labour now has more members than the Conservatives, the Liberal Democrats, and the SNP combined. The enlarged full-time membership of 350,000 will contribute £8m to Labour in membership fees. If Labour were able to increase its membership still more it would free itself from the need to rely on any external funding whether from trade unions or individual donors. The influx of new members has brought a new radicalism, purpose and clarity to the party. It has raised the possibility of Labour becoming a movement again, developing a new creative tension between the party's representative role and its movement role. It has drawn a definitive line under the New Labour era, ensuring a sharp break. Whatever comes after Corbynism will not be a continuation of New Labour in any of its forms. All wings of the party after Corbyn are forced to imagine themselves anew. This will aid the process of renewal.

But the negatives are also powerful. Jeremy Corbyn's victory brings back an old Labour problem, the split between its membership and its MPs, which Richard Crossman reflected on in the 1950s. Crossman argued that the members were always much further left than the leadership and the majority of the MPs. The trade unions were a counterbalance to the membership which allowed the leadership to control the party and the conference and determine policy. Leaders were elected by MPs, which was a further safeguard. The MPs twice elected a leftwinger as leader: George Lansbury and Michael Foot were the two clearest examples, but no leftwinger has ever lasted long as leader or succeeded in being elected as prime minister.

Corbyn is novel precisely because his authority does not rest at all upon the support of his MPs. But in a parliamentary system that is a crucial weakness, and is already raising serious questions over the viability of his leadership and how long it can last. The difficulty for Labour is that under their new election rules if the MPs decided to trigger a new leadership election at some point in the next five years the membership might well just re-elect Jeremy Corbyn. The MPs may find it very difficult to work with him because of their disagreement on many fundamental policies, but they will be stuck with him until the next election unless opinion in the party shifts.

Now that he has won Corbyn's problem is how to unite the party, bridge the gulf that has opened up between the MPs who have their mandate from the voters and the members who expect him to deliver a radical alternative, and at the same time reach out to all those voters who did not vote Labour last May. Two views can be discerned within the Corbyn camp. There are those who think the only solution to the split between the members and the parliamentary Labour party (PLP) is to change the PLP. The party rules must be amended to make deselection of sitting MPs easier, to purge the "Blairite virus" from the party as one trade union leader put it. At the same time policymaking would be made subject to the consent of all party members in a bid to win support for some of Corbyn's policy positions and put pressure on MPs to support him.

For this to be possible Corbyn's supporters would need to gain control of the national executive committee, the party headquarters and the party conference. The main obstacle to this strategy is that it would likely lead to a full-scale civil war in the party and could not be made to work quickly. MPs can be deselected but they would stay as MPs until the next general election in 2020. A party visibly at war with itself is likely to see its poll ratings drop sharply. Corbyn has appointed a broad-based shadow cabinet, but precisely because it is broad-based the majority of its members disagree with him on fundamental issues and he has already climbed down on several of them, including agreeing that the UK will remain in Nato and agreeing to campaign for Britain to stay in the EU regardless of the terms Cameron negotiates.

The alternative strategy is for Corbyn to seek to build a much more inclusive movement, embracing not just those who have supported him in the leadership election, but also the other wings of the party, and many groups at present outside the party. This pluralist strategy would mean that Corbyn would agree to compromises on policy to keep the PLP behind him, but would aim to shift the party on to a different trajectory in the long term. It is probably much easier for him to win broader support on domestic issues, particularly the construction of an anti-austerity programme, than on foreign policy issues. His problem is that there are some foreign policy issues, such as military intervention in Syria, and renewal of Trident, which he feels so strongly about that it will be very hard for him to compromise, and his authority will be undermined if he does. He already risks being seen as a prisoner of the PLP and his shadow cabinet, and it will be very hard for him to create a positive image of his leadership for the wider electorate. The first polls show him with the kind of negative ratings which Ed Miliband had to endure for most of his leadership. But Miliband at least started off with positive ratings. Corbyn has begun with negative ones. It will be very difficult for him to climb back from that.

Many of his supporters argue that this does not matter, because the aim of his leadership is not to win the election in 2020, but to stake out new ground, shift the political debate, and change the Labour party permanently. On this view Labour has embarked on a journey which will take at least a decade to bear fruit and possibly two. Behind this strategy lies a deep rejection of the representative politics which Labour has practised for a century, because it means giving up the ambition to win power in the British state and implementing policies and reforms that can improve conditions for the majority of citizens. Instead the goal becomes a long slow process of cultural transformation, gradually increasing the strength of social movements allied to Labour which are anti-austerity, anti-capitalist, and anti-war. Staying true to principles is more important than making compromises to win power. These are two very different conceptions of politics.

THE FUTURE OF THE LABOUR PARTY

Any viable social democratic politics for the future is going to have to find a way to bring principles and power back together. Unless being leader changes him radically, Corbyn's politics is a dead end for Labour and is likely to result in an even more decisive defeat than in 2015. But charting an alternative is far from easy, not least because of the structural predicament Labour finds itself in, along with most other European social democratic parties. The heart of this predicament is that Labour has come to be in a different place from most voters, and often appears as a relic of the industrial age. The party is measurably weaker than it was in the 1970s. Trade union membership has been halved, manufacturing industry and working-class communities have declined, collectivist attitudes have weakened. The "world of Labour" which GDH Cole wrote about a century ago is a shadow of what it was. It is not coming back. Members of trade unions are only 25 per cent of those in employment and only 14 per cent of workers in the private sector belong to unions. In the public sector that rises to 55 per cent, but even that only amounts to three million workers, and public sector employment is shrinking under the present government. Fifty per cent of workers now work in small and medium-sized enterprises, and 15 per cent are self-employed, three times as many as those in minimum-wage jobs.

Labour has to compete in this new space. One of the key questions facing it is whether it should aspire to be a catch-all party again, or whether it should set its ambitions lower. Can it ever again assemble a great national coalition of interests, groups and regions as it did in 1945, 1964, and 1997? Can it ever aspire to get more than 40 per cent of the vote again, which it has only ever done in six general elections since 1918? Britain has increasingly become a multi-party system in general elections, but the first-past-the-post system converts that multi-party system into the familiar two-party system in Westminster. This exaggerates the strength of the two main parties, and forces both of them to maintain the pretence of being catch-all parties in order to get into government. But it is increasingly clear that neither are, least of all Labour. If there had been a proportional electoral system at the last election the result would have been: Conservatives 256 (instead of 330); Labour 200 (instead of 232); Ukip 85 (instead of one); the Liberal Democrats 50 (instead of eight); the SNP 25 (instead of 56); and the Greens 20 (instead of one).

Accepting that Britain is now a multi-party system and should have an electoral system which reflects that should be an essential aim for a new progressive politics. Once such a system is achieved both Labour and the Conservatives might well divide into more than one party, as is common in many other parts of Europe. A second aim for a new progressive politics has been well stated by Jon Cruddas, who observed that Labour only wins when it has a unifying and compelling national popular story to tell.[3] It had such a story in 1945, 1964 and 1997. One of the strengths of Corbyn's campaign for the leadership was that he did communicate a vision and a purpose. He suggested at one point that Labour should re-adopt its old clause IV, with its commitment to full socialisation of the economy. But it is a vision and a purpose which belong to a different era.

The third aim for a progressive politics is to devise a substantive programme which can inspire and energise, but also persuade people that high principles, strong commitments, and grassroots democracies can be joined to a strategy for power and governing. The choice between representative politics and grassroots politics is a false choice. There has to be a creative tension between the two if progressive politics is to renew itself. Across Europe social democracy has been on the defensive in recent times. Since the financial crash centre-right parties have tended to be in the ascendancy in many countries, and the established parties have been challenged by new populist insurgencies. Social democratic parties have become too comfortable, too safe, too remote. They have to reconnect with new sources of energy and excitement. They have to inspire people. Social democrats have to learn how to become insurgents again, and engage with the myriad of groups across civil society which aspire to govern themselves and to shape policy.

BECOMING INSURGENTS AGAIN

If there are three principles which can frame such an enterprise the first is a commitment to developing a new view of what a progressive or reformed or civic capitalism could look like.[4] There are many ideas to draw on, radical challenging ideas, such as those put forward by Matthew Taylor[5] or Charles Leadbeater.[6] We need new formulations of how to make socialist values compatible with market effectiveness, how to achieve a dynamic, entrepreneurial, innovating economy, encouraging the new emerging sectors – such as online, automation, clean energy, and life science. We need an industrial strategy which promotes a sharing economy, mutualism and ethical practice, new forms of finance and crowdfunding. We need new ways to govern and regulate markets, which include radical policies which challenge some of the abuses of property rights which distort markets and lead to rising inequality.

A second principle is to restate the vision of social security for all and what this means in our current political economy. The aim of creating a high-trust, socially cohesive society remains paramount. The task of a new progressive politics is to find the best ways to achieve that and counter the strong trends making for higher inequality in incomes, in wealth, in life chances and in gender roles, tackling the formidable challenges of demography, affordability, and secular stagnation which threaten the viability of welfare states everywhere.

A third principle is interdependence. One of the most important features of our world for the last 200 years has been its increasing interdependence. Progressive politics will not succeed anywhere unless progressives ally with one another to help strengthen the institutions of global governance, most of which from the EU to the UN are in a fairly parlous state right now. We need more global cooperation, not less, if we are to address any of the big challenges from migration to climate change which confront us.

Politics always in the end disappoints and frustrates. But it is also a perennial source of hope, imagination and new beginnings. Those of us committed to progressive politics need to begin to explore what such a new beginning might look like.

NOTES

1. Diamond, P. & Radice, G. (2015) *Can Labour Win? The Hard Road to Power*, London: Rowman & Littlefield International, http://www.policy-network.net/publications/4963/Can-Labour-Win.

2. Keeble, S. & Straw, W. (2015) *Never Again: Lessons from Labour's Key Seats*, http://www.fabians.org.uk/publications/never-again-lessons-from-labours-key-seats/.

3. Helm, T. (2015) 'Jon Cruddas: This could be the greatest crisis the Labour party has ever faced', *The Guardian*, http://www.theguardian.com/politics/2015/may/16/labour-great-crisis-ever.

4. SPERI. 'Civic capitalism research', http://speri.dept.shef.ac.uk/tag/civic-capitalism/.

5. Taylor, M. (2015) 'Grasping the future – why progressives must champion the human potential of the digital economy', *Royal Society for the encouragement of Arts, Manufactures and Commerce*, https://www.thersa.org/discover/publications-and-articles/matthew-taylor-blog/2015/09/grasping-the-future--why-progressives-must-champion-the-human-potential-of-the-digital-economy/.

6. Leadbeater, C. (2015) 'Imaginative ideas that could save the Labour party', *The Guardian*, http://www.theguardian.com/politics/2015/jul/12/14-ideas-that-could-save-labour.